A Hooker's Guide to Getting A Job

FISH HOOK BOOKS, LTD.

www.fishhookbooks.com

A Hooker's Guide to Getting A Job

Parables from the Real World
of Career Counseling and Executive Recruiting

BRUCE A. HURWITZ, PH.D.

FISH HOOK BOOKS, LTD.

A Publication of

Fish Hook Books, Ltd.

www.fishhookbooks.com

Copyright 2012 Fish Hook Books, Ltd.

All rights reserved.

Library of Congress Cataloging-in-Publication Data

Hurwitz, Bruce A.

A Hooker's Guide to Getting a Job : Parables from the Real World of Career Counseling and Executive Recruiting / Bruce A. Hurwitz. – 1st ed.

ISBN-13: 978-0615622217

ISBN-10: 0615622216

Ten percent of all revenue from the sale of this book will be donated to non-profits supporting veterans.

TABLE OF CONTENTS

ACKNOWLEDGMENTS

WHILE MEETING TO DISCUSS social networking, I told my friend Gil Effron, the marketing wizard behind *How to Give Your Business an Extreme Marketing Makeover* and 10daymarketingmakeover.com, about the history of this book's title. He made the convincing observation that some people might find it offensive. He then came up with the initial concept for the cover, a man sitting on a fish hook. The fish hook logo puts things in their proper perspective as the intent of the book is to hook you on my approach to conducting an effective job search, while hopefully putting a smile on your face. I cannot properly express my appreciation to him for his insights and suggestions.

I am also grateful to Bob Conrad of Conrad Communications who did the actual final design of the cover and facilitated the production of the book.

Finally, much thanks to Christel Hall for her editing and proofreading prowess.

While I am delighted to share with them credit for any success, the responsibility for the content – and the inevitable typos – is mine and mine alone.

—B.A.H.

PREFACE

THE IDEA FOR THIS book first came to me when I remembered a guest speaker (I forget his name or profession), who visited us during my senior year of high school. When I began high school a different gentleman had told us, "Study whatever you want, but not accounting. There are too many accountants. You'll never find work." Senior year's guest told us, "Think about studying accounting in college; there aren't enough accountants!"

But he said something else: "Regardless of what you study, when you go to look for a job, think like a hooker." I, and my fellow students, all laughed. Our teacher? Not so much. But our guest explained:

"Think about it this way. A hooker needs to know how to market herself, negotiate a verbal contract, close the deal, and have customer satisfaction to get repeat business and referrals. And that's what you need to do when looking for a job."

OK. That is not a direct quote. But it's the spirit of what he said and the source of the title. As for the source of the subtitle, that comes from Danny Cahill's book *Harper's Rules: A Recruiter's Guide to Finding a Dream Job and the Right Relationship*. (Danny was a guest on my radio show, *Bruce Hurwitz Presents* – www.brucehurwitzpresents.com). Technically it's not the subtitle, it's the "pre-title," if there is such a thing. At the very top of the cover page is written "A Business Parable." It's a great book, which, in fact, I assigned to my Professional Development class at the Mechanics' Institute of the General Society of Mechanics and Tradesmen of the City of New York. My students, without their knowledge, were the guinea pigs for this book and the lessons herein offered. I thank them for their insightful questions and the Institute's director, James Loriega, for the opportunity to teach at the 150-year old institution.

The stories that make up this book, while parables, works of fiction, are nevertheless totally accurate portrayals of my career counseling clients, executive recruitment candidates, audience members at the various speeches I have delivered on the subject of conducting an effective job search, or conversations I have had with colleagues. So a word of warning: if you think you recognize yourself or someone else in this book, you are mistaken. All the stories are composites of real people, not actual individuals. And if the name of an employer happens to be the name of a real company or non-profit, it's purely coincidental. The lessons are real. The explanations are real. The conversations are truthful recreations of combinations of actual interviews I have conducted or about which I have been informed by the interviewer or interviewee. Everything else is pure fiction.

Each chapter features a different fictitious character: the woman thinking about quitting her job; the man who has been laid off; the college grad. In each case we will learn from their experiences. After all, it's better to learn from someone else's mistakes than from your own. And, for that matter, it's even better to learn from others' successes so you can try to replicate them!

In the book I referenced above, Danny uses one fictional character and the lessons he offers are powerful. However, how can a 55-year-old man who has just been laid off relate to a thirty-four-year-old woman, Danny's character, who has just quit her job? Or, for that matter, how can a 23-year-old recent college graduate relate to either of them? Accordingly, my approach is to give examples that will resonate with all readers, both on a personal level (because they are the same gender, have the same marital status or are in the same age group) and more generally as well (because they are going through the same thing as is the character).

There are four parts to this book. In Part One I look at different scenarios for how people find themselves unemployed and what they do about it. In Part Two, the focus is on a plan of action for getting the next job. In Part Three, we learn about failing and succeeding at the interview. And in Part Four we consider two special groups, recent college graduates and veterans. In the concluding chapter, Lesson Learned, I recap all the lessons found in the book. As you'll notice, the main lessons are highlighted at the conclusion of each chapter.

Let's get back to our hooker – and, for the record, I have never utilized the services of practitioners of the world's oldest profession – because that's the approach I really do take when conducting a job search, although this is the first time I am publicly admitting it! (I was once going to tell the story to a group that I was speaking to on the topic of cover letters and résumés. My friend, who was also speaking at the event and who had arranged my participation, advised against it. For some reason he thought telling a room full of women to use prostitutes as their role model for finding a job would not go over well…!)

Remember the quote? "Think about it this way, a hooker needs to know how to market herself, negotiate a verbal contract, close the deal, and have customer satisfaction to get new business and referrals. And that's what you need to do when looking for a job." Marketing yourself. Negotiating. Closing the deal. Customer satisfaction.

New Business. Referrals. All key components of an effective job search.

As a job seeker you need to know how to market yourself. The most effective way to find a job is through networking. You need to be at the right place at the right time. You have to know where to go and how to approach people. You need to know how to dress and what to say.

As a job seeker you need to know how to negotiate a contract. You need to know what you want, understand what the employer needs, how to effectively get your message across, and how to clearly establish expectations regarding the actual work to be performed and the compensation to be paid.

Finally, as a job seeker you need to know how to close the deal, meaning how to deliver on your promises. Today's job is a stepping stone to tomorrow's. Your new boss will hopefully be a referral source for a future employment opportunity. And your supervisors will be your references, so you have to keep them all happy, satisfied and content.

So perhaps the analogy is not as silly as you might have first thought. And one thing is for sure, you'll never forget it!

Please keep in mind that I try not to repeat myself throughout the various chapters. Once I have established a rule, for example, that networking is the key to finding a job, I see no reason to recount telling each subsequent individual the same thing. (Sometimes I will, for the continuity of the story.) In that regard, it is important for you to read the entire book to get the full picture of my approach to finding and securing employment.

That said, here is the key to my approach and what I believe truly distinguishes me from the vast majority of career counselors:

First, there are what I call "The Two Great Anomalies." Here's the first one: Your job search has nothing to do with you. That's right; you are incidental to the process. The only person who matters is the person doing the hiring. What you want does not matter. What the employer wants is the only thing that counts. That's why, as you will read, starting a résumé with an "Objective" or a "Professional Summary," is at best silly and at worst an insult to the intelligence of the recipient. You have to meet the employer's needs; she doesn't have to meet yours!

(Yes, you are correct. The employer does have to meet your compensation and professional requirements. But that is only after she has decided to offer you the job. That's the negotiating phase. Then it is about both of you. Until then, it's all about the employer!)

Here's the second "Great Anomaly." When I make a formal presentation I have a handout that describes it this way:

Days/Weeks/Minutes

vs.

Seconds/Seconds/Hours

A job seeker will spends days working on his cover letter. He'll spend weeks working on his résumé. But he'll only spend minutes – maybe an hour – preparing for an interview. Yet an employer will spend only a few seconds on a cover letter, even less time on a résumé that does not grab her attention (and then maybe only a minute scanning), but hours on an interview. This includes the time of all the staff members who meet with candidates and the time they spend together discussing the candidates. So instead of trying to create the perfect cover letter and the perfect résumé, candidates should prepare for the perfect interview.

And finally, the key to getting a job is differentiation. You have to differentiate yourself from your competition. If I have succeeded in writing a book worth the time and money you are spending on it, then by the end you will know exactly how to do that.

Feel free to let me know if I have succeeded or failed. You can send me an e-mail to bh@fishhookbooks. com. I always value hearing from readers. I will respond as quickly as possible to all inquiries. Your questions and my answers will make up a future volume of *A Hooker's Guide.*

And by all means, visit the 'Courses' page of my corporate website, www.hsstaffing.com. There you will find a number of videos, the majority of which are free, dealing with various job search and professional development issues.

Best of luck with your job search, and thank you!

Bruce Hurwitz
February, 2012
New York, NY
bh@fishhookbooks.com

PART ONE: BEING UNEMPLOYED

LET'S BEGIN WITH THE beginning. People find themselves in need of a job for any number of reasons. They need a change. They were laid off. They were fired. They are moving.

Whatever the reason, they have baggage to deal with. In the coming chapters we will look at how real people cope with real issues of unemployment.

CHAPTER ONE:
Take This Job and Shove It!

REMEMBER THE JET BLUE flight attendant who supposedly cursed out the passengers, grabbed a couple of beers, opened the door, released the emergency slide and ran away to fame and fortune? Well, he got fame but not fortune.

Everyone, and I mean everyone, had to have felt the same way at some point in their career: I wish I had done that! It's human nature. Of course, once the security camera footage was released and it became clear that he almost killed someone when he released the slide, it wasn't so funny anymore. There's a limit and he passed it. You don't want to burn bridges but you do want to feel better about yourself. That's why you want to quit. You're miserable. The question is, why?

There could be a number of reasons: You hate your boss. You hate your co-workers. You hate your customers or clients. You may love them all, but hate your commute. Or it might just be that you hate your job or your career. Or you just might want a change.

When Rita came to me she was visibly distressed. An attractive woman, I estimated to be in her late 30s – early 40s (although whenever an executive recruiting client asks me how old a female candidate is I always say, "All the women I interview are 29," at which point they realize they asked an illegal and stupid question and move on!), came to me looking for direction. She did not know what she wanted, only that she wanted a change.

My approach, especially in this economy, is that now more than ever, you don't want to quit your job until

9

you have a concrete offer in hand. So we had to discover what the problem truly was.

Prior to meeting with me, I send career counseling clients a long list of questions. It's not homework. They don't have to prepare written answers. I make it clear to them that all they have to do is think about the answers. It helps to put them in the proper mindset for our meeting. Questions like:

What steps have you already taken in your job search? What made you decide on career counseling? What did you want to be when you were a child? What influence does your family have on your job search? What influence do friends have on your job search? What influence does your culture have on your job search? What influence do your values have on your job search? What do you want? What or who is holding you back? Skills? Qualifications? Training? Experience? Contacts? Knowledge? Motivation? Self-confidence? Money? Support? What problem(s) are you facing? What have you done to alleviate them? What are your goals? What have you done to reach them? What is your style? How do you reach decisions? Are you "process oriented" or "results oriented?" What do you daydream about when you are at work? What work atmosphere do you most enjoy? How do you cope with stress? When did you overcome adversity? How will you know that this consultation was a good idea? How do you learn? On the job? Research? What book are you currently reading? What magazines do you regularly read? What do you think about? Are you analytical? Emotional? Creative? What do you need to make you happy? Leadership? Control? Influence? Helping others? A team? Isolation?

Challenges? Conformity? Security? Risk taking? Money? Status? What clubs do you belong to? Would you be open to part-time, contract assignments, consulting, freelance work, franchise opportunities, or self-employment?

"Bruce, I really appreciate those questions. They got me thinking."

"Thanks. I'd like to take credit but I stole them from a number of authors!

"But tell me, what have you been thinking most about since you reviewed the questions?"

"I'm confused. I don't know what I want."

"No problem. I've seen your résumé, but tell me about yourself."

(You see, people define themselves by their work. Or to be more exact, Americans define themselves by their work. When we meet someone for the first time, we have no problem asking, "What do you do?" We not only do not consider it rude, we consider it polite. But in some cultures it is, in fact, considered very rude. So if Rita answers with anything other than her profession, it should be an indicator that she needs a new career. Otherwise, it might be that she needs a new job or new responsibilities.)

"I'm a financial analyst. I've been working for City National for six years and, as you see, I've worked my way up the ladder. I'm a senior financial analyst supervising more junior financial analysts than anyone else."

"Do you like them?"

"Love them!"

"Continue."

"I'm the first one in the door in the morning and the last one to leave."

"Rita, I wear two hats. I'm an executive recruiter and a career counselor. Since you have come to me as a career counselor and not as an executive recruiter, the rules of the game are different. I can ask you questions that legally I am prohibited to ask as a recruiter. However, that said, I'm going to forget your answer if I have a candidate who is looking for someone with your qualifications. So with that understanding, do I have your permission to ask whatever I want?"

"Shoot!"

"Are you married?"

"I knew you were going to ask me that!

"No, but even though I am Latina and wearing a cross..."

"For the record, I did not ask you about race and religion!"

"...I have a 'Jewish mother' who is nagging me about grandchildren."

"And I'm not so stupid as to ask you how old you are although I can guess from the résumé!

"But enough illegalities, why are you 'first in and last out?'"

"Because I love my work. I fall asleep when I hit the pillow and wake up every morning before the alarm. I get to the gym, work out for a good hour, rush home, shower, get dressed, eat and jump on the subway. I'm only three stops from my office door. If it's raining or snowing, I don't even need an umbrella. The subway station is right at the corner of my block and right at the entrance to my office building. So I'm a groundhog when I'm commuting."

"May I be blunt?"

"Absolutely. I'm not paying you to be my friend; I want 'blunt.'"

"What the hell are you doing here? You clearly love your job and your co-workers. You have not mentioned your boss so I assume she...

"He!"

"...he is not the problem. You beam when you talk about work. You came in looking like I was about to give you root canal without anesthesia, and now the color has returned to your face, you're smiling and seem to be totally relaxed. And, and this for me is key, you have no difficulty falling asleep or waking up. So what's the problem?"

"It's silly."

"If it caused you to pay me $250.00 to come and sit in my office for an hour, hour and a half, two hours, so that I can help you come up with an effective career plan, it may be a lot of things, but it ain't 'silly!'"

"I'm bored!"

"Why is that silly?"

"I'm earning $200,000 plus bonus; I love my co-workers; I have no family issues..."

"Not even with a 'Jewish' Latina Catholic mother? Sorry."

"Don't be funny! I'm paying YOU, remember?

"...no family issues; good friends; and a great Manhattan apartment and, yes, it's rent controlled!"

"OK, you win, it's silly. But it's still real. Something is missing. Let's find out what it is.

"When I look at a résumé, one of the first things I look at is years of employment. You have had three jobs over the past ten years. The first, fresh out of graduate school – Columbia? Couldn't get into an accredited college? – was for two; then the Savings and Loan for three; and now going on six at City National. You are not, what we call, a 'jumper.' You have a good résumé. You stay a reasonable time with an employer and in each job, and new position, you have advanced. So your career is not an issue. You are in great shape."

"I know..."

"Alright. If you would like to waste time and money, I know a couple of people, and I actually like one of them, who conduct aptitude tests for a living. They – the tests, not the people – are idiotic. I took them both. I paid nothing for them and they were worth every penny. They won't be worth what they'll charge you! One is so bad that in the introductory letter that comes with the test results it literally states, 'The test results may be wrong. You should ask people who know you best what they think.' That's not a quote, but it's close enough. So let me save you some time and money:

"If I were to ask your mother and best friends what would they tell me about you?"

"The truth?"

"No, I want you to lie. It makes the time go by quicker."

"I love numbers; I love gadgets; I love analyzing situations and proposing solutions."

"Great. Just because you love doing something does not mean you are good at it. How do you know you're good at it?"

"You saw my résumé. If I was no good, would I be earning what I'm earning and working where I'm working and have the responsibilities that I have?"

"Nope. I knew that. I just wanted to make certain that YOU knew it."

"I know it."

"All right. So you love numbers, gadgets, analysis and proposing solutions. Do you get to do them all in your present job?"

"Absolutely!"

"You didn't say you 'love working with people?'"

"Don't turn into a psychologist. I know your Ph.D. is in International Relations!"

"True. But you didn't say it."

"I meant it. I love our customers. I love our vendors. I love supervising people. I love seeing colleagues grow professionally. That's what I meant before by 'I love my coworkers.'"

"OK. So what's missing?"

"That's..."

"That was a rhetorical question. I was asking myself! Here's one for you: When was the last time you were proud of yourself?"

"How are you with financial data, economics, statistics and the like?"

"If my friends and a few former professors were in the room, they would be on the floor laughing."

"OK. This is what happened in terms a Ph.D. in International Relations can understand."

"Thank you!"

"You're welcome!"

"The bank was looking to increase revenue through a new investment policy. We wanted to see what would happen if we changed how we invested and the new policy, whatever it was, had been in effect ten years ago."

"Clear enough. You created a program that would run ten years' worth of investments based on ten years' worth of data. If it would have worked from 2001 to 2010, you would be confident that it would work from 2011 to 2020."

"Very good, Doctor."

"Piled Higher and Deeper, Ms. MBA."

"Fine. So I created the program, I ran the numbers and the first proposal would have been a disaster. The second would have been even worse. Then my assistant had an idea. The little rat came up with the solution.

"I took her with me to the boss. I told him how great I was for hiring her and, without telling her I was going to do it because I did not want her to panic..."

"You're a good supervisor!"

"Thank you, I know, and don't interrupt because I am getting to the good part ... I told her to present the idea. She did. I presented the results and the boss took us both to lunch."

"He's a good supervisor."

"He knows. Don't interrupt. I'm getting to the good part.

"We got back to the office and there was a message that his boss wanted to see him. Turns out the Board got wind of the suggestion to change the investment strategy and they nixed it. 'The economy is too volatile,' they said."

"Do I really have to tell you what the problem is?"

"Look, I have a great boss. I understand how the game is played. My supervisees respect me. I'm a big girl. Today they say 'no,' tomorrow they say 'yes.' If nothing else, we designed a great program that we will be able to use when meeting with clients to show them what we could have done for them had they been banking with us since Day One."

"I'm surprised that software did not already exist."

"For that purpose, it does. But what we designed was much more complicated than that."

"Too complicated for a Ph.D. in International Relations to understand?

"I didn't say that!"

"When was the last time you got to implement one of your proposals? To see it through to fruition? To use a sport's analogy, to take the ball and run with it?"

"Very rarely."

"Bingo!"

"What-o?"

"*That's what's missing. You don't want to change careers, employers or co-workers. And you don't want more money. You want more responsibility.*

"*I had the same problem twice. I was the chief fundraiser for a Jewish Federation and was bored to death. Intellectually stimulating it was not. All we did was an annual campaign. Anyone whose honest, mature, and knows what follow-through is can do it. No problem.*

"*I wanted more. So I convinced the boss to make me responsible for Planned Giving, meaning charitable investments...*"

"*That's not exactly what Planned Giving is!*"

"*Don't interrupt. I'm trying to make it comprehensible for an MBA from Columbia.*

"*So I proposed a Planned Giving department. I wrote up the proposal, he submitted it to the Board, and they approved it. All I wanted was a title change; I didn't ask for more money. My first boss taught me that the money will follow, the important thing is to get the responsibility.*

"*The second time was when I was the chief fundraiser for a nursing home. After a while I was again bored to death. I also had responsibility for marketing and PR. I convinced them we should have a live cable television show for which I would get corporate sponsors. They agreed. I got a bank to sponsor the show. And I had a ball hosting and producing it!*

"*You need to go to your boss and tell him that you want more responsibilities. You need your Planned Giving program or television show. The question is, what should it be?*"

"*I don't know how to respond?*"

"*What's the process at the bank when you have finished your analysis and presented your proposal?*"

"*My boss reviews it. Usually he accepts the proposal, sometimes with modifications.*"

"Nothing wrong with that. That's what he gets paid for."

"Correct. So once he is on board, he takes it to his boss, the executive vice president, who signs off on it. It's not pro forma. He knows his stuff and usually makes a few insightful suggestions."

"So far, so good."

"Then it goes to El Presidenté. And, no, there's no hidden issue with my using my Spanish. It's just a joke."

"I didn't say anything."

"You were thinking it!

"And then THE PRESIDENT signs off on it. And, if necessary, he'll bring it to the Board."

"Then what happens?"

"It goes to the EVP who gives it back to whoever gave it to him. And then that person gives it to the worker bees to implement."

"How many such proposals or projects are going on at any one time?"

"Half a dozen?"

"Does anyone oversee their progress?"

"The individual supervisor."

"Don't you mean, the individual supervisors – plural? There could be as many as six."

"Yeah. So?"

"What if there was a department for new proposals? Looking at everything at once? Making sure that everything made sense in the bigger picture? That there was proper coordination?"

"That would be fun..."

"And what if that was your new – additional – responsibility?"

"That would be nice. But how do I sell it?"

"Well, I'm only a Ph.D. in International Relations, but I would suggest a three-page proposal explaining how in the past – and here I am obviously making an assumption – a lack of project coordination cost the bank money or opportunity. Can't you go back and make a project analysis the way you make financial analyses?"

"I could do that..."

"And would those new responsibilities make you happy? Get you excited? Get you out of my office so I can go to lunch?"

"Yup!"

"Send me the draft. Don't worry that I won't understand the technical stuff, I just want to proofread it."

It worked. Rita got the new job. She did not ask for a raise or a new title. But they gave them to her. On her own time she created the case for what became her new position. Since she was not asking for a new title, there was no need to worry about the organizational chart. Since she was not asking for a raise, budgetary issues did not come into play. Her plan was so persuasive that the Board bypassed all the bureaucracy and just did the right thing.

The important thing to note is that Rita now has what she was missing. If she had quit her job it would have been totally unnecessary.

The lesson here is, sometimes you need to build on the strong foundation you have already built, not start something new. In other words, a new job is not necessarily the answer. Sometimes all it takes is thinking about what is missing at work and finding a cost-effective way to fill it that benefits you and your employer. That's what Rita did.

CHAPTER TWO:
We're Sorry,
But We Have to Let You Go.

RIGHTEOUS INDIGNATION IS THE only way I can think to describe the emotions of far too many people who contact me to tell me that they have been laid off through no fault of their own. While I want to help them and enjoy helping them, I dread the appointment because I know that it will be two hours long and the first half hour will be a venting session. In some cases, truth be told, that's all the person needs or wants. So I sit and listen. My pre-appointment questions are irrelevant and these people really don't want to discuss cover letters and résumés, let alone interviewing and negotiating.

And that could be a problem, because if they have been employed for many years, they may have forgotten how to conduct a job search and especially how to interview. They have been sitting too long on the employer's side of the table. The transition to the other side is difficult.

But that was not the case with Richard. It became clear fairly early in our interview that all he needed was someone to listen to him and reassure him.

"Richard, have a seat. Can I get you something to drink?"

"Thanks and no thanks. I appreciate your seeing me on such short notice."

"No problem. My pleasure – well, not really given the circumstances. Twenty years with the same employer. What happened?"

"I feel like an idiot. I just did not see it coming."

"Forget about the clock. I've reserved two hours for you."

"But I thought it was an hour-long session?"

"It is, but I flunked kindergarten and can't tell time. So don't worry about it. Just start at the beginning and explain to me what happened."

"This was my first job out of college. Is that going to be a problem?"

"I'll answer your question but from then on just tell me the story.

"The answer is that it will be and it won't be. You are not what we call a 'jumper' so you'll be able to present yourself as someone who is loyal. Employers like that. However, you have only worked at one place and therefore only know how to do things one way. That may be a problem. But there is a simple way to get around it. You were with one employer but worked at different divisions. If you present each division as the equivalent of a separate entity, that means you have had a good half dozen different work environments – supervisors, colleagues, products, etc. – and that should put employers' minds at ease when they consider you. As I like to say, 'The good news is you have had one employer for 20 years. The bad news is you've had one employer for 20 years!'

"Now get back to the story. What happened?"

"When I graduated college, on graduation day, I walked into Penn Station wearing my gown and did not notice the police woman standing by the stairs. I was day dreaming and bumped right into her. The next thing I heard was barking. She was with the K-9 unit and her canine partner was not happy.

"I froze, apologized profusely and took a step behind her – even though the dog was on the leash and it was clear to his human handler that I had not attacked her.

"She was very nice, as were BOTH her partners – human and canine! We chatted for a minute and I turned to get to my gate and my future boss was standing there smiling. I asked him what was so funny and he told me that he liked my style. He said that he liked the fact that I had apologized, didn't make excuses, and stayed cool and calm under pressure. Remember, I had the presence of mind to put the police woman between me and the dog.

"I thanked him and he gave me his business card. He told me to call him when I was finished day dreaming and came down to earth. I couldn't believe the coincidence; he was an architect!

"That was the start of a ten-year long business relationship and friendship. I called him the next Monday and he invited me in for an interview. I didn't even have a résumé. We chatted and he offered me a job. So I almost literally worked my way up to a vice presidency from the mail room.

"As you saw from my résumé – first one in twenty years! – I got my Bachelor's in Architecture and my Master's in Art History. My passion is old buildings. He hired me to help in the Sales department. He told me that it was the best way to learn the business.

"He was right. For two years I interacted with customers and potential customers. I learned what they wanted. I learned what they did not want. I learned how to speak with them.

"I guess I should have explained; A & C Architecture specializes in remodeling. We can remodel anything. And we do it without demo. In other words, we go in and save the client money because we don't demolish everything. It's cost effective and few firms do it. They make the case that it's easier to go in, knock everything inside the four walls down and start from scratch. We take a different approach. Maybe one wall has to come down, but it's incidental to the project. Bottom line is most

of our clients are small businesses. Like the retail shops on the main floor of this building. But we have had some major chains as well, like drug stores, looking to modernize their stores.

"In any case, I worked my way up and was constantly being given new responsibilities."

"For the record, you have had an excellent career and have a great résumé. I know plenty of people who would kill for what you had. But continue."

"Thanks. But nothing succeeds like success and success attracts buyers. And we got bought out. The boss made it clear, everyone had to keep their jobs, compensation packages, responsibilities, authority. And the new owners honored that commitment. They were great.

"But, as I said, nothing succeeds like success and they sold because of the economy. The offer was too good to be true. The owners just could not turn it down, even though we were going to become just another office of the new agency, not a separate entity.

"The deal was very generous and all employees with over five years tenure received a bonus, on the condition that we signed a statement that we had quit our jobs and were now applying to the new company for employment and would not hold the new owners liable for any grievances we had with the former owners. It was supposed to be pro forma. *Life was to have continued as usual. And it did, for a while.*

"A few months ago, things started to change. People were being transferred to the main office near Wall Street. Everyone who was transferred performed a function that did not exist in the Wall Street office. The rest of us, who had similar responsibilities to some people downtown, remained. And then it happened.

"The new boss called us all together for a meeting. He apologized, blamed the economy, and handed us severance

packages. The checks were generous and if we accepted them we had to agree not to sue. He left the room and we all discussed it, even though it was not an 'all or none' proposition. But we all agreed that it was best to take the money.

"The entire process took less than a year. The former owners never saw it coming and we certainly didn't."

"You were laid off; you were not fired. In today's economy everyone understands that and no one will blame you for it. It will not be held against you.

"The other good news is, you have money so you can afford to be unemployed – albeit for a little while.

"Since you are meeting with me as a career counselor I can ask this: Tell me about your family."

"I'm married to the same woman for the past 15 years. We have one 13-year-old who is about to turn 30. She wants to be a graphic designer. My wife is the executive assistant to the president of a jewelry manufacturing company."

"Do you have health insurance?"

"We will continue to get it through the old company – I have to get used to saying that! – for the next six months. Then, if I'm still unemployed, my wife's company can provide the coverage."

"Good. So you have money, I assume, for the next six months, meaning your severance will cover you, and you don't have to worry about health insurance."

"Correct."

"So, what I want you to do is to take your wife and daughter back to where it all began, Penn Station. But first book three tickets on Amtrak and a hotel somewhere – preferably where the train will be stopping."

"Very funny!"

"Thanks and, by the way, I'm serious. A flight these days is too stressful. For better or worse, there's no 'real'

security on Amtrak so you don't have the, for lack of a better word, 'craziness' of an airport. And train travel is relaxing. Once you arrive, grab a cab and go to the hotel. Before you book, make certain they have what you will need – free Internet, restaurants within walking distance, a fitness center, a pool, whatever. When I'm stressed I go to Fredericksburg, Virginia. If I remember correctly it's only six hours away. There's an Econo Lodge with all the amenities, and last time I was there it only cost me about $50 a night. It's relaxing and inexpensive. You need to take a couple days to recharge your batteries and put things in perspective.

"You don't know it, but you are not in bad shape. You have not been complaining about your wife and daughter, so I will assume you have no family problems."

"Correct."

"Your standard of living is guaranteed for half a year and you have a wife earning a full-time salary. You are not going to have difficulty paying your mortgage, although you may have to set priorities."

"I'm listening."

"And the big thing, health insurance, isn't an issue – and your daughter's tuition payments are a few years off."

"Thank God!"

"And I think the fact that you now have some color in your face is a sign that you agree with my analysis."

"I do."

"So let's get started. I'll talk, you write. Agreed?"

"Go ahead."

"When you get back from vacation, you have to tell the world that you were laid off and that you are looking for a job. If you don't, it means you don't have a network. No network; no job. Contacting only a portion of your network means reducing your chances of finding a job by the same percentage.

It's a zero sum game. That means everyone you know: family, friends, old school chums, former colleagues, church members, your minister, members of any clubs you belong to, and even the vendors you use every week like the dry cleaner."

"The dry cleaner?"

"Yes, they hear things; and have your daughter tell her best friends."

"Be serious."

"True story. Father got laid off. He was a CFO. Daughter's best friend's father was looking to hire a controller. Daughter asked father for a copy of his résumé. Daughter gave résumé to best friend. Best friend gave résumé to her father, who called the girl's father, who got hired. When I say 'everyone,' I mean 'everyone.'"

"Point taken."

"The secondary reason for the vacation is that you have to make certain that when you start networking you don't come across as bitter. When you start networking, don't even discuss what happened. Keep it simple: 'New owners let all of us go. Now I'm looking for my next twenty-year opportunity!' The key is not to sound bitter because no one is going to help a bitter person find a job. It will reflect poorly on them.

"Think of it this way. Your friend Joe gets you an interview at his company or at a friend's company. You go in and spend most of the time complaining about how unjust the world is. You leave and Joe gets a call from his boss or his friend: 'Why in the world would I want to hire a guy that's bitter? Are you nuts?' You destroyed Joe's credibility. He's not going to help you again. Get my point?"

"Got it."

"My guess is that you will find a job by networking. Don't forget vendors, the people who used to provide you with services – like the copier guy – because they visit offices and hear

things. It's not as crazy as it sounds. And, of course, clients. There's nothing wrong with calling past clients, so do it."

"In the meantime, Google 'executive recruiters architects,' and get your résumé out to all of them. It can't hurt."

"Is my résumé OK?"

"Yes, it's OK, but OK isn't good enough. I want to make a suggestion.

"Most résumé recipients don't spend more than a few seconds looking at them, so it's key to grab their attention right off the bat.

"Start the résumé with a 'Selected Accomplishments' section. List, in bullet-points, five or six things that you have done most recently that will resonate with architectural firms. The first point, which will be the most powerful, you should also use in a cover letter. But in your case, I don't think you are going to need a cover letter because I honestly believe you'll find a job through your network."

"Why?"

"This may sound contradictory, and I know I'm repeating myself, but you come across as a bit hurt but not bitter. And unlike some people I've met with, you still come across as professional. You are not taking things personally. You know it's just business. When clients take things personally, they usually have a great deal of trouble finding the next job. They simply radiate, if that's the right word, negativity. No one is going to hire them until they stop feeling sorry for themselves. They are worse than people who get fired. At least when you're fired, you pretty much acknowledge on some level that it was your fault, but when you're laid off, and it comes as a total surprise, they have to blame someone so they harp on the past instead of focusing on the future."

"So why am I not harping?"

"Because you have a good support network – your wife and daughter."

"How do you know?"

"Trust me, if they weren't quality, you'd be complaining about them. But, you aren't complaining about anyone. You haven't even cursed out the new owners of the company."

"Maybe I'm about to go postal!"

"Just don't do it here! I actually like my office neighbors. But feel free to come to my house."

"Don't like those neighbors?"

"Let's just say I believe in high fences and I don't have any fences at all!"

"So what else do I need to do with my résumé?"

"Nothing. It's fine the way it is. But make certain to send me the final draft and draft cover letters, so that I can review them."

"All included in the fee?"

"All included in the fee. And, I almost forgot. Call me before you have an interview and after the interview so we can strategize."

Sometimes it all comes down to a gut feeling. There was something about Richard that told me he was respected. He was stressed but remained professional. He looked me straight in the eye. He didn't exaggerate or spin the facts. He knew he had nothing of which to be ashamed and spoke with confidence.

I'm far from perfect, but in this case I was right. A couple of weeks later, after finalizing his résumé, he went to lunch with an old friend who just happened to be friends with an architect. They had not spoken in years, but Richard was comfortable calling him. He was not embarrassed about reaching out to someone with whom he had not kept in touch.

His friend was delighted to reconnect and to be of assistance. Sure enough, Richard got the interview and the job. Granted, it was a smaller shop and he was earning less, but he was still making a good living and his self-worth was improved immensely since he was only unemployed for a matter of weeks, not months.

But I did warn him of one thing. He had only had one employer for close to 20 years and only knew how to do things the old company's way. I told him never to utter the words, "Well, at A & C we would..." but to say out loud, "Explain to me how you do it here." He called me after he had been working a couple of days to tell me that he kept reminding himself of those instructions whenever he was about to criticize.

That attitude carried the day. His new boss and colleagues recognized that he wanted to be part of THEIR team and not make them part of HIS team. They liked and respected him and I have no doubt he'll be with the new firm for another 20 years!

The lessons here are simple: network with everyone you know and attitude is everything.

CHAPTER THREE:
You're Fired!

HOW DO YOU DEAL with a gap on a résumé?

That's a question that comes up very often. For whatever reason, many people left the traditional job force for an extended period. The good news, as noted previously, is that most recipients of résumés only spend a few seconds looking them over, so they sometimes miss some red flags. And the reddest of all red flags is an employment gap.

I received from a candidate a résumé which had on it, "CEO, Mom, Inc." It was a good résumé. I called her for a preliminary phone interview and asked her to tell me about "Mom, Inc." She said, "I've been raising my kids for the past 12 years." While it was cute, I told her to get rid of it. She was rightly hesitant because she was afraid of the gap.

The solution I proposed was to put "Housewife" or "Homemaker" or whatever term made her comfortable. Then to list all of the responsibilities and skills she had learned over the years: calendar management; negotiations; budget oversight; interacting with healthcare providers; maneuvering through local, state and federal bureaucracies; public relations; etc. She laughed, but got the point and made the changes. She called me back a couple of months later and told me that she had had some interviews and was starting her new job the following day.

Another frequent gap is for being a caregiver for an elderly loved one. Again, I recommend putting

"Caregiver" on the résumé and listing the skills: personal assistant, maneuvering the health care bureaucracy, evaluating non-profit senior services providers, etc. That does the trick.

The point is that not having been in the (traditional) workforce for a number of years for "care" reasons is nothing about which to be ashamed. What can be more admirable than raising children or taking care of an elderly loved one? It will certainly resonate with the interviewer. And, if nothing else, it shows that you have learned patience! More importantly, it sends the message that the kids are old enough to take care of themselves or that the issue with the parent is, sadly, over. In other words, there will be no personal distractions in the work place!

The key is to tell the truth, don't play games, and highlight what you learned from the experience. This is especially true in the case of a negative.

What happens when the gap is the result of incarceration? Same thing - with one difference: don't put it on your résumé. Explain it in the cover letter – something I only recommend in this case. (I discuss cover letters in detail in Chapter Eight.)

There are three reasons why you have to let the employer know and, by the way, it is illegal to discriminate against persons who have been incarcerated. The first reason is that convicted felons are not permitted to work in some industries, such as healthcare and finance. (I once had a non-profit client that helped abused women. They were willing to consider non-violent felons.) Second, they are going to find out about it anyway, so if you are upfront with them they will give you a point for being honest. And finally, the issue really isn't what you did but what you learned. So explain what you learned from the experience and why it makes you a better employee.

Admitting the truth, and focusing on lessons learned, is also the case when you have been fired. And that's even true if you are as big a low-life as Michael.

"Thanks for agreeing to see me. I really appreciate it."

"My pleasure, Michael. I was impressed with your résumé."

"Thanks. I've had a good career and am now focused on the next advancement."

"I like your use of the word 'advancement.' It appears from a review of your résumé that you have advanced in all of your positions and each move to a new employer has been a step up the professional ladder."

"That was the plan all along. My father's a big planner. All of us kids, the day after we graduated, had to present him with a business plan. We were the businesses and we had to stick to the plan. If we deviated we had to be able to justify it to him!"

"Sounds like a strict but caring man."

"He was."

"Was?"

"He passed away a while ago."

"My condolences."

"Thanks. It was especially hard, surprisingly enough, on my wife and six-year-old son. They were very close."

"Well it's nice that your son will have warm memories of his grandfather. So tell me about your work."

"It's pretty straight forward. I'm a marketer. Started in sales and worked my way up to what is now called 'Business Development.' But it's all really just sales. I got tired and walked

across the hall to Marketing. Turned out I am pretty good at selling product but even better at promoting the company."

"That's a great description of sales vs. marketing."

"It's better than the text books!"

"So why are you here?"

"Well, I want to remain in marketing but I've gotten all of my jobs through clients. In other words, a client would hire me, I'd go work for him, and then a few years later I'd leave to join a different client. This is the first time that I have ever been 'between' jobs, as they say."

"So what made you decide to leave your job at – Bryson, Inc.? – without having something in hand."

"Yeah, it was Bryson. We sell various types of software. I'd be happy to tell you about their products."

"No need. Continue. So why did you leave?"

"As I said before, my father passed away. It was very hard for me. We had been close. Simply put, I lost focus."

"It happens. I had one executive recruitment candidate for a fundraising position in Cleveland. No, it was in Chicago. His father was in Cleveland, very ill. He was looking for work to be closer to his father because he was living in California. The closest he could find work was Chicago. Not great but certainly not bad. As he was driving up to Chicago, he got a call that his father had passed away. He called his new boss, explained the situation to her, continued on to Cleveland and did what he had to do.

"Two weeks later he was at work and absolutely miserable. He did not have his support system. He felt totally alone. His work was OK but not what they had expected. And he, too, was not happy with his performance. So he quit. I had no problem submitting him to my client. Everyone totally understood and appreciated the situation he was in. In fact, his Chicago boss even provided a warm recommendation.

"*The point is, family tragedy is, sadly, a great reason to leave a job or even to fail at a new job. It's understood and no one will hold it against you.*

"*I don't have to tell you that the best way to find a job is by networking. After all, based on what you said, networking is how you got all your jobs. So why not get on the phone and call past clients, colleagues, friends, relatives, whomever and get the network working for you?*"

"*That's just it. Maybe it's time for a change. Maybe I need something totally new.*"

"*But you said, not five minutes ago, that you wanted to stay in marketing.*"

"*I know. But I just think this might be the opportunity to maybe do something new. I must have transferrable skills.*"

(Even though the alarms were ringing and the red lights were flashing, I decided to play along. An inconsistency like this – "I want to stay in marketing" vs. "I want something new" – almost always points to, at best, deception, at worse, an outright lie.)

"*Alright. Let me ask you some questions.*

"*First, when was the last time you were proud of yourself?*"

"*I take it you mean professionally, because I was very proud of my son at my dad's funeral.*"

"*Professionally.*"

"*I'll spare you the details, but we developed a new software package. Imagine a suite of programs for engineers akin to Microsoft Office.*"

"*Seems logical.*"

"*But surprisingly a hard sale and things were not going well. We couldn't figure out why.*

"Against everyone's advice, and I'm not exaggerating by much, I hired a kid fresh out of school. He had zero experience. It was all potential. But he had that certain something and my gut just told me that he would be a great producer.

"He had only been working for us for a few months when he came into my office. His mother was with him. He wanted to introduce her to me or me to her. After the normal pleasantries he asked me if something was bothering me. I told him the Xylon project. Don't ask! I don't take responsibility for product names.

"In any case, he said he was going to walk his mother out and then he'd be happy to come back and help.

"He returned a little while later and I showed him the data. We track everything. If it's quantifiable, we quantify it. If we can't quantify it, we don't care about it.

"I noticed on your LinkedIn profile that you have published a few things."

"A few."

"So you know that if you proofread something over and over again, after a while you are no longer reading what you are seeing but what you remember. In other words, you can't see it anymore."

"Truer words have never been spoken."

"Well, it was the same thing for me. I had been looking at the stats for so long I was no longer picking up the important trends. Mark pretty much took one pass over the material and started asking insightful questions. He found what I had missed."

"And you were proud because…?"

"I was the one who hired him. I pulled rank, said it was my team and everyone gave in. And he proved me right. So I was proud of him and, quite frankly, proud of myself."

"I'd suggest teaching but…"

"Tried it. Waste of time. No one is hiring. Years ago the city would hire anyone without a criminal record interested in teaching. All you needed, I think, was a B.A. Today, with the unions, budgets and I don't know what, that program is dead."

"So if teaching is out, supervision is in."

"Are you asking me or telling me?"

"Both."

"I guess you are correct, but what industry?"

"Looking at your résumé I see that you are now in IT. You had previously been in food, hospitality, and business services. There's almost a logical progression here. So I guess the question is, what comes after IT?"

"Don't know."

"Would you like something to drink?"

"Water would be nice."

"I'll go get some for both of us and in the meantime you think about what comes after IT."

***

"So? What comes after IT?"

"Healthcare."

"Because everything is being digitalized?"

"Yup!"

"Logical. So who do you know that's involved with clinics, hospitals, doctors' offices, nursing homes, hospices, assisted living facilities, etc.?"

"I don't know."

"Let's check. I know you are on LinkedIn. Log onto your account – just make certain you don't accidentally save the password! You know what, just to be on the safe side, use the 'Private Browsing' option."

"Good idea and I'm in."

"OK. Go to your Inbox and click on 'Compose Message.' See the blue 'In' icon? Click on it. Now click on the dropdown

menu under 'Industries' and look for 'Healthcare.'

"There's 'Health, Wellness and Fitness' and 'Hospital and Health Care.'"

"Hospital and Health Care."

"OK. Now what?"

"How many contacts do you have?"

"Seventy-five."

"Great! That's your core network."

"Some are out of area."

"Who cares? They may know someone around here. Today, geography means nothing. When you get home, send them all a nice message that you are looking for your next opportunity and will be happy to share with them your résumé."

"To be totally honest, I would be uncomfortable reaching out to them."

"Everyone has things that make them uncomfortable. Personally, I hate going to parties or events where I don't know anyone. I dread having to introduce myself to strangers."

"That's not my problem."

"Everyone is different. We all have our quirks. I'll pretty much do anything to get out of going to a party but I have no problem speaking to an audience of 500 strangers. Go figure! So what IS your problem?"

"I'm very well known in my industry and if someone wanted to help me they would have. But it's been weeks and no one has contacted me. I have a feeling that I'm going to have to start from scratch."

"I don't follow. Look, I have over 30,000 first-degree contacts on LinkedIn. I may personally know a few dozen. And I doubt many more than that actually know me or of me. Of those 75, how many do you actually know?"

"None. But I'm still hesitant to reach out."

"Don't be.

"What does your wife say about all of this? Especially the fact that you quit your job without having a solid offer."

"To be perfectly honest, following my dad's death we had some hard times. She took our son and moved in with her mother."

"I see."

"So your network has folded on you and your wife has left you. Since you said, 'to be perfectly honest,' let me ask you a question: Why did you leave your last job?"

"It was time for a change."

"Did you resign?"

"No."

"Were you fired?"

(After a minute of staring at his cup of water and the floor…)

"Yes."

"This time tell me the truth. If you lie I can't help you, and I guarantee you won't get a good offer. Employers neither hire nor keep liars."

"My father died. I hated the man. My wife and son loved him and were talking about how much they missed him. He was great to them and terrible to me. I was glad he was dead and I resented her reaction and, to some extent, his – my son's. They could not understand that he was a phony. He treated them one way and me the exact opposite.

"So there was tension in the house. This was the time that Mark introduced me to his mother. Turns out, she worked nearby and we ate lunch at the same diner. Of course, before he introduced us we didn't know each other. The next time I went for lunch, not every day you understand, she was there. We sat together and started a friendship.

"We were both having issues with our spouses. One thing led to another and we started meeting after work. You can guess the rest."

"OK. So how were you discovered?

"Mark has a girl friend. Her father owns some motels and is looking to expand. He invited Mark's father to partner with him in an initial real estate deal – purchasing a motel, just to see if they could work together. One Saturday Mark and his father were checking out a motel that was for sale. When his mother and I walked out of our room he and his father were standing right there. If they had planned it they could not have timed it better."

"And then what happened."

"He and his father stared at both of us and said nothing. When Margaret, that's Mark's mother, got home her husband was packing her clothes. He threw her out. Turns out they had a pre-nup. Adultery results in eviction from the family home. Period. Nothing to discuss.

"She called her sister, told her what happened, and her sister refused to take her in. My wife, Sally, had already moved out so Margaret moved in."

"Your wife didn't know about the affair?"

"She never said anything but I think she suspected. In any case, Mark called in sick and the following day went straight to the company's CEO and handed him a resignation letter. The CEO took one look at it, told him he was not the one leaving and came down to my office.

"He showed me the letter and asked me if it was true. When I confirmed it, he cursed me out, called for boxes and security, and had me thrown out. The company has a morals clause in its employment contract. It's hard to enforce. They told us it's like Justice Stewart's definition of porn, 'I may not *be able to define it, but I know it when I see it.' This was 'it,' no question about it."*

"So basically what you are telling me is that everyone who knows you, everyone in your industry, knows what you did and won't have anything to do with you. You are not going to get any references. You are basically on your own and no one gives a damn. That about right?

"Yup."

"You were fired for cause. You're scum. And you can't hide."

"Yup."

"OK. Not my place to judge but suffice it to say, you have to aim very low."

"How low?"

"Telemarketing and professional coaching."

"That low?"

"That low."

"Telemarketing I get. What do you mean by 'professional coaching?'"

"I had a couple of bosses at a non-profit many years ago. Something bothered me about them so I quit. I didn't know what was happening but I knew something wasn't kosher. Sure enough, a few years later they pleaded guilty to grand larceny. I don't know what happened to the exec but the assistant exec became a professional coach, or some such thing. I saw him on the news once and could not believe it. Here this crook was giving professional advice to businessmen and women. I went to his website and conveniently he had left a few things out of his bio.

"Let me give you another example. I have had phenomenal luck getting press coverage. I'm in the media on average three times a week."

"I noticed that on your website."

"Yes, I'm quite proud of it actually. In any case, I give PR/media consultations and speak on the subject of how to get free PR to grow a business. One of the participants at one of my presentations called me. I asked her what she did and she told me she was a Ph.D. in 'Wellness Sciences' or some such thing. But she also said, 'Oh, I do a lot of different things. I'm also a certified yoga instructor!'

"She was all over the place. Very disorganized in her thinking. I'm prejudiced in favor of my fellow Ph.D.s and naively believe that while we are not all brilliant we at least know how to put together a sentence or two. So when she came up for air I asked her where she got her doctorate.

"She told me and continued talking. I started typing. Turned out her college was unaccredited.

"When she took a breath I stopped her. I told her that she did not have to be defensive but she needed to realize that if I suspected something was not right reporters might as well. And just as I now know she does not have a legitimate doctorate, the press may also find out and publicize it. So she should think twice before looking for publicity. I never heard from her again.

"And for my radio show, a similar thing happened. In this case, the so-called 'Ph.D.' actually listed her college on her website. I told her I would be happy to interview her on my show but I would have to ask her about having an unaccredited degree. I also never heard from her again!

"My point is this, people don't always investigate. We are a trusting species. Yes, the truth might – and probably will – come out. People looking for a coach don't do criminal background checks and people going to experts assume that their degrees are legitimate.

"In the short-term, your behavior is going to cost you.

But if you tell the truth, or at least don't lie, you should be alright.

"What this means is that if you are asked why you left your job you don't say 'I had an affair with a colleague's mother.' You say, 'Following the death of my father I had a serious lapse in judgment. Nothing criminal but it cost me dearly. While there are always two sides to every story, I make no excuses. In any event, I learned an important and costly lesson so you are now speaking with someone who values morals, ethics, and decency above all else. No one is harder on me than me! I don't compromise on my principles anymore.'"

"So what do I do?"

"You start from scratch. If you like the idea of helping people to overcome adversity – and I know you like supervising – then look into becoming a certified coach. Go to networking events. Hustle for clients the way you did at the beginning of your career. Bottom line, you have burned and buried all of your bridges. You might even want to leave town."

Rarely have I ever disliked a client as much as I disliked Michael. And I thought about whether or not I should even help him. For better or worse, I decided it's not my place to judge. So I gave him my honest opinion.

After their divorces were finalized, Michael and Margaret got married and moved. It took a good year and both of them were working low-wage jobs. Because of the terms of the pre-nup, Margaret was not entitled to anything and, of course, Michael had to pay alimony and child support. So times were tough but that brought them together.

In their new home, in a new city, in a new state, where no one knew them, they started over. Margaret got a job as a secretary at a small IT company. Michael had been taking an on-line coaching course and got certified. He hung out his shingle and, when last I heard, was making a living.

In case I need to say it, the lesson here is, be a decent human being and always remember, as the saying goes, "It's not the crime that kills you, it's the cover-up!" Oh, and DON'T LIE!

CHAPTER FOUR:
There's Always an Excuse – Too Old, Too Young...

WHEN I AM WEARING my executive recruiter's hat, I like people who make excuses. They are easy to work with. It's called "self-fulfilling prophecy." If you come into my office and tell me that you will never get a job because you're ____ (fill in the bank), I pretty much am willing to guarantee that you are correct. Nothing succeeds like low expectations. Since you don't want to be disappointed, tell everyone you are going to fail. When you do you will have the satisfaction of being able to tell everyone that you were right and you knew it all along. A self-fulfilling prophecy at its best!

So, congratulations! You were right! Of course, you're still unemployed but you have the satisfaction of clairvoyance. And, most importantly, I don't have to waste my time with you!

A lady in her late fifties, early sixties, came to my office for career counseling (so I had to waste my time with her!). It was not so much that she was "old" that was her concern, but rather that she had not been able to find a job for seven years. This was before the economy took a tumble. The bad economy just exasperated things.

She had had an impressive career in media. She had won awards in television and radio and seemed to know everyone. She regularly went out with well-known radio and television hosts and producers. Naively, I thought her case would be easy.

Let's call her "Mary." When Mary first contacted me it was in a long, well-written e-mail, explaining to me the present state of the media industry. It was wholly negative. But her résumé looked good. I figured she had been laid off from her most recent job – not realizing that her résumé misrepresented her employment history. She had had some short-term consulting/project assignments, but in any 12-month period, was more unemployed than employed.

When she arrived, I complimented her on her analysis of the media industry and on her résumé. She basically told me that I did not know what I was talking about (and, since the résumé misrepresented her actual work history, she was right). According to her, none of it meant anything. There were no jobs. She would never be hired again.

And she was adamant about it. No one was interested in her. She was a has-been!

I asked her to tell me about her career. She treated me to half an hour of old boss badmouthing. (That's the one thing that will always kill an interview. If you badmouth a past or present employer or colleague in an interview, the interviewer will figure you'll be badmouthing him if he hires you and you leave under less-than-ideal circumstances. So why hire you?) Everyone had always been out to get her and they had finally succeeded. Her bosses knew nothing and would not listen to her. So she basically failed everywhere, even though she had had some successes.

Still not realizing that she had, for all intents and purposes, been unemployed for seven years, I asked her about her network. She started name dropping. When I asked if those celebrities would help her, she said some had gotten her part-time gigs (at this point she explained/

clarified her résumé), but basically they just told her that the market was awful and they couldn't help.

With Mary it was clear that there was a problem with her network. If she really knew all of those "names," and I had no reason not to believe her, then the question was, "Why were they not helping her get full-time employment?"

The answer, after an hour and a half of total negativity, was that Mary, to quote countless kindergarten teachers, "does not play well with others." She is a nightmare to supervise. Her friends did not want to stick their necks out for her. She would embarrass them.

It did not matter what ideas I threw out, Mary would dismiss them with a "Tried that," or the ever popular, "It won't work."

Finally, I asked her what was missing? She told me, among other things, that she was not current on the latest technologies. "So why don't you take a course?" "No point," she replied, "even if I knew how to use the software I won't meet the minimum number of years' experience."

Always an excuse...

Mary was a career counseling client. Alice, on the other hand, was a potential candidate for one of my executive recruiting clients. She had sent me her résumé a while back and I now had a candidate looking for someone with her qualifications.

When she arrived, she looked "old." Granted, she had probably seen 60, but I know plenty of 60-year-olds who don't look (or for that matter, act) their age. She looked 60 and then some. She also was carrying three bags. That did not help. She looked like a stereotypical "old bag lady."

Alice is a great case study for what not to do in an interview. She did so many things absolutely wrong. (I'm intentionally not telling what the job was I wanted her for because it's irrelevant. This is about attitude, not qualifications.)

First off, she was late for the appointment. Granted, it was only a few minutes, but still, she was late. She should have apologized.

Second, as noted, she came across as a bag lady. Those three bags, along with her disheveled appearance, made her seem "old" regardless of her age. She looked like someone who was just going through the motions.

Third, as soon as we sat down her cell phone went off. She apologized and said that she had thought she had placed it on vibrate. The phone should have been off. After all, you can still hear a cell phone vibrate, and what is the point of having it vibrate if you shouldn't be answering it at all?

And fourth, she could not find the cell phone to turn it off. That made her appear disorganized.

But her biggest mistake was her attitude.

I complimented her on her résumé. She dismissed my compliments, pointing out that she was "too old and have not had a job in three years." I responded that I had a job that I thought she would be perfect for and told her to start focusing on the future, not on the past.

I then explained to her that the client was looking for someone who was a decisive decision maker. Someone who could analyze a situation, identify the problems, come up with solutions and implement them with minimal supervision. She said she could do that.

We chatted for a while, and then I told her they were looking for someone with energy. I told her that when I first saw her with all those bags she looked disorganized and that she should not carry more than one bag.

At that she became agitated. "I need these bags. This is New York City. I have to have a bag for my shoes. I wear sneakers when I'm walking around town and put on nice shoes for interviews."

I then knew there were going to be problems. First, she did not take criticism well. Second, she could not see the obvious solution – a small bag for the shoes that she could place in a larger bag. And third, once she became defensive, the negativity increased.

It became clear to me that she probably did not want any job but was just going through the motions. She was trying to convince me that she was not a good candidate and that the client would not want her.

Then she told me about her financial problems. That was my opening. I told her that the salary would be at least $75,000 and that would go a long way toward solving her financial problems. She then responded, "Well, you want me to make changes in my résumé. I can't do that because I can't afford high-speed Internet. At home all I have is dial-up. I pay $10 a month for it and may have to cancel that as well."

I told her that I did not understand the problem since she could send me the updated résumé using a slow Internet connection. After all, it was only a document.

"Well, I can't use the phone and Internet at the same time and I don't want to be on the Internet during the day in case I get a call regarding a job!"

You can't make this stuff up!

I reminded her that she was having, with me, an actual job interview and that I thought she would make a good candidate for my client. Granted, at that point I was probably trying to convince myself, but I knew my clients and I thought they might go for her if I could turn her around. I then added that she could e-mail me the résumé that night and that I would submit her the next day.

She then told me that I could submit her, but she would not agree to an interview without first speaking to her career counselor.

That for me was the end. Three years with no job and she's paying a career counselor! I asked her how long she knew her. When she told me, "Since the day I lost my job," I suggested that she should save her money. She responded, "Oh! I can't do that. I can't fire her. We've become friends."

I wanted to tell her that she didn't need friends, she needed a job, but I knew she was beyond help. I did tell her that I would not submit her unless she promised me she would go for an interview and seriously consider the position if offered. She promised to think about it and call me by Monday morning.

This was on a Tuesday. When I got back to my computer I had an e-mail from a LinkedIn connection whom I had contacted about the job. He told me that he was not interested but that his wife might be. I called her and Wednesday morning she was in my office.

She was smart, young, attractive, fresh out of school, had a great attitude and was absolutely unqualified for the position. She had had some internship experience and that was it.

But I knew my client. I called him up, told him about her, told him that she would take a low salary (I had, in fact, told her to forget about the salary range listed on the job description. The lowest was too high for her!), and that she could start right away. This would be a hire based on potential, not experience.

I had to do a little arm twisting, but he met with her first thing the next morning and she started that Monday. When Alice called to tell me she did not want the job, I told her it was alright and that the position had been filled by another candidate.

Telling her was a judgment call. I wanted her to know that the position was real and that she missed out on a serious opportunity. And I also told her that I thought she would make a good candidate in the future and that she should stay in touch. All she said was, "No point. No one will hire me."

So much for Alice.

Two candidates who applied for the same job came in with a similar concern, but not an excuse. Like Alice, they were not career counseling clients but rather candidates for a position with one of my executive recruiting clients. It was not, therefore, a meeting about some future possible job, how to find it and how to apply, but an interview for a real job which the employer wanted to fill ASAP. Neither of these gentlemen was employed.

On August 10, 2011, I gave a talk at The New York Public Library on "How to Conduct an Effective Job Search." One of the participants asked me if I had seen an article in *The New York Times* about employers refusing to hire the unemployed. I told her that I had not. I asked her how many employers were quoted. She said "a few." Someone else said "half a dozen."

My response was that *The Times* has an agenda. They want President Obama reelected. Everyone knows that unemployment is going to be the main issue in the election. If they can deflect blame from Mr. Obama's policies and focus the spotlight on mean employers who won't hire the unemployed, they will be serving him well.

I also knew the report was wrong because my clients tell me that they are more than happy to consider the unemployed. They realize that it is a "buyers' market" and that they are the "buyers." You can get great people for a modest price. It may not sound nice, but it's true.

Apparently, I convinced my audience that there was no real story since they dropped the issue. Then on October 7, 2011, if I remember correctly, Fox News Channel had a segment on *Special Report* that confirmed *The Times* story. Now let's be honest, if Fox is confirming what *The Times* has reported, it's either true or life as we know it is about to come to an end!

But what Fox reported was a bit different. They correctly reported that many states are making it illegal to discriminate against the unemployed. And they had a "fair and balanced" discussion about the pros and cons of creating a new "protected group" of individuals, akin to members of a particular race, religion, etc. But they also said that in all of their research they could find only 110 companies posting Internet ads for positions for which "presently employed" was a qualification for consideration. Do the math: 110 out of hundreds of thousands of employers advertising on the Internet does not seem worth bothering about.

I stand by my statement, although I'll insert a caveat: with the exception of an infinitesimal number of employers, employers are willing to consider the unemployed. They do not discriminate. They would be foolish to do so. It costs more to "steal" an employee from an employer than to hire an unemployed person. End of discussion.

As I said, neither of these fellows was employed. One was in his early sixties; the other, in his late twenties. They were concerned about their ages, not their employment status. The fact that I met with both of them within a span of two days, and they were the only ones I submitted to my client, makes it a good case study on assumed age discrimination.

The position was director of marketing for a non-profit in the Bronx, New York. (For the record, while this is a fictionalized account of an interview, it is, in fact, how I actually conduct interviews. In that regard, it is an accurate depiction of an interview by an executive recruiter, me, with a candidate for an actual position. You'll notice I never ask the candidate what he wants. That's because I do not work for the candidates, I work for my clients. I'm only interested in what my clients want. It's my job to see if the candidate is a match. Only tangentially do I inquire about the candidate's wants since if things do not work out with the present client, the candidate might be suitable for a future client. In any case, I know what my candidates want, a job!)

"Sam, come on in."

"Pleasure to meet you."

"Pleasure to get your résumé! It's not every day I have a résumé from someone who has worked for IDEO, Ogilvy and national non-profits. So the pleasure is mine."

"Usually they say a résumé should only be one or two pages long."

"That's usually said by people who get paid to prepare résumés that are one or two pages long. My response is simple: people read Who Moved My Cheese? which is probably only about 75 pages, and yet they will also read Gone with the Wind and War and Peace. It's content and interest, not length. You have seven pages of content and it's an interesting read!"

"Thanks."

"Let me explain how the game is played. The role of the cover letter is to get the recipient to read the résumé. I'm your cover letter. I contact the client, send them a report on our meeting along with your résumé, and get them to read the résumé. If all goes well, you get an interview."

"Seems like a good process."

"It is, as long as you keep me in the loop. The advantage of working with a recruiter is that I advocate on your behalf. You are not just seven pieces of paper stapled together in a pile of a hundred résumés. You are one of only a few and, as far as I can, I nag them about you.

"But let's get started."

"What do you need to know."

"OK. What's the best way to reach you?"

"Cell is best."

"718-555-1236?"

"1237."

"Ah, that's why I begin with the contact information. Trust me on this one. You are not alone. Many people don't bother to proofread their contact information and that's where the error usually is. We would have found it sooner if I had tried to call you instead of sending an e-mail."

"Am I still a viable candidate?"

"If I rejected candidates for typos on their résumés I wouldn't have many candidates. Don't worry about. I'll correct my copy, you correct yours.

"The lawyers say I have to ask everyone the same way: Do you have a permit to work in the U.S.?"

"Born and raised."

"What are you currently earning?"

"Eighty-five thousand plus pension, full healthcare and a month's vacation. I never get sick and never use personal days and, frankly, I don't know how many I have."

"I forget. How did I find you?"

"LinkedIn. You're connected to Joe and Joe put me in touch with you."

"Joe gets a cookie."

"Actually, if I get the job he says it will be a steak dinner!"

"Let's hope Joe has a good meal in his future.

"Not related to any job in particular, is on-the-job travel a problem for you and would you be willing to relocate?"

"Travel is OK, but not more than 25-30% and, no, I can't relocate."

"Now when I submit a candidate I prepare what I call a 'Submission Document.' It has three sections. The first is 'Rationale for Submission.' I explain why I think you are a viable candidate. It's more subjective than objective. The second is 'Summary of Interview,' and the third is your résumé.

"So let's get down to business."

"One word answer, but if you need three you can have three. And I don't ask trick questions. What's your profession?"

"I'm a marketer."

"Good answer. Every so often someone surprises me and I don't like to be surprised. I was once interviewing a woman for a fundraising position at a non-profit. She had been a fundraiser for 20 years, primarily within the Jewish community. When I asked her that question she said, 'social worker.' That pretty much meant that she would not be a good fit for a non-Jewish non-profit. You see, for historic reasons, and happily it's *beginning to change, Jewish non-profits hire social workers for pretty much all positions. It's a mindset that would not work in a non-Jewish organization."*

"How do you know?"

"Fifteen-to-twenty years experience with non-profits, both Jewish and non. And I never let my prejudices get in the way. Even though I knew it would not work, I still submitted her to a client, she got the interview, but they very diplomatically told me that she lacked 'the proper attitude.' I learned my lesson."

"Just curious; what was the best answer you ever received?"

"A fundraiser said, 'Storyteller.' Perfect answer.

"But I digress. What do you like about your work? Professionally, what do you enjoy doing?"

"I like being part of the decision-making process, especially the implementation phase. Someone comes up with an idea, we sit around and discuss it, we agree on whatever we agree on, and then it's my job to market it to the community. I have to put it in terms that the general public will understand and appreciate. That's the challenge and I love challenges. I also like working with really smart people.

"I don't know if this matters…"

"It all matters!"

"…but I also like utilizing technologies. I don't just mean social media, but mass e-mailing (NOT SPAM!) to members, and having exciting things for people to do on our website; that kind of thing."

"Anything else?"

"Nope. That's about it."

"OK. I told you that the second part of my Submission Document is a summary of this interview. I will frame the discussion about your candidacy around your answer to this

question. Give me some examples, and tell me where, of successes you have had of which you are particularly proud."

"When I was with Ellis, we decided to launch a new program for seniors – bulk mail preparation. A lot of senior service organizations, even nursing homes, have an 'Industry Division,' for lack of a better term. Residents or clients are given real jobs, at the facility, for real clients."

"Say no more. I worked at two nursing homes and we had a large program at the first one. Mailings. Packaging. And some more things I don't remember."

"Packaging?"

"Yeah. Clients would hire us – funny how I still say 'us' – to put together packages for them. Think about the instruction booklets, warranties and the like that come with any large piece of electronics that you buy. That sort of thing."

"I'll steal that idea."

"It's yours. I guarantee you that we stole it from somebody else. That's how the game is played!"

"In any case, we started a bulk mailing program. We would stuff the envelopes and then organize them for bulk mailings. We hired an expert. You see..."

"Stop right there. I worked for non-profits in the States from 1991 to 2003. Believe me, I KNOW POSTAL REGS! I can tell you horror stories. No need to tell me!"

"So our expert would oversee everything and our clients would do the work, including Alzheimer's clients – depending on the stage of the disease."

"Great plan."

"But you understand it because you worked at nursing homes and know what Alzheimer's patients/clients can do. Most people think they are crazy, so I had to market workers with Alzheimer's to prospective clients."

"And you were successful?"

"In my first month I brought in two clients. They were small jobs. But then one of them recommended us to one of their competitors and the other came back to us with a larger project. All of a sudden we were getting referrals and had more business than we could handle. Then we had the problem of UBIT. You know?"

"Ah, my friend, you are bringing back warm memories. 'Unrelated Business Income Tax.' You are a non-profit serving seniors. The mailing program is therapeutic in nature. Now it is becoming a real business. It's all fine and good as long as the workers are seniors or have Alzheimer's..."

"'Or?'"

"Yeah. We had one Alzheimer's patient who was in her late thirties. It's rare but it happens.

"...but now you have to outsource some of the work. And you are outsourcing to mailing houses that have idle workers and are willing to do the work at a discount. They are not non-profits. So is just the income you make from the work you farm out subject to UBIT or have you contaminated, so to speak, the entire program and it's all subject to UBIT?"

"And we pay the lawyers to work it out. In other words, nothing succeeds like success. So if we are paying UBIT, it might not be worth continuing with the program. Or, we could just take on the amount of work we can handle, in which case, I marketed myself out of a job."

"OK. Give me something else. One more will suffice."

"At UNB we had an HR director who didn't quite understand the concept of 'confidentiality.' If you wanted a rumor spread, she was the person to tell it to.

"No one trusted her, except the EVP and CEO. They loved her. They would not even listen to complaints about her. If someone went to her to discuss an issue with a supervisor, she *would call the supervisor almost before the employee had left her office. She was awful.*

"Of course, sooner or later, it all falls apart. One of the staff – IT WASN'T ME! – said to her, in passing, something like 'Sheila and Paul' – the EVP and CEO – 'seem to be getting really close.' In and of itself, a phrase pregnant with possibilities. Of course, she took it to mean romance and set the rumor mill spinning. And she got caught."

"OK. We have all had to deal with company gossips and they usually meet the same fate. What does this have to do with marketing?"

"Nothing as such, but in order to replace her we would obviously need a new HR director. She was the chair of the local HR association branch. She knew everyone. So we had to come up with a way to get rid of her without her being able to sabotage us. It was given to me to come up with a strategy."

"You have my attention."

"First, I wanted to see how bad it would be. So I called a few HR directors, all with healthcare/non-profit/senior services experience to see if any of them would call our HR director. I might have made six calls before my phone rang. Kate, that's the HR director, was on the line. She wanted to know why I was making inquiries about HR directors, and she was mad.

"I told her that I planned to speak to her at the staff meeting that was scheduled for later that day. I said that I was a volunteer for a non-profit that was conducting a confidential search for their first HR director and, of course, was planning to ask her for any recommendations.

"That was also exactly what I had told the HR directors. So it was really a game of telephone. She actually thought I, the director of Marketing, was asked to find a replacement for her! Someone had actually told her that. I couldn't believe it.

"*The one piece of information I had to have, and the CEO gave me, was her salary information. So once she calmed down I said something like, 'The problem is, they are only willing to pay...' and I made up a sum about 15% higher than her salary.*

"*She immediately said that she might know of someone and wanted to know which non-profit it was.*

"*I told her it was confidential and not even definite that they were going to hire someone. I made it clear to her that there was no job as of yet, and might not be one.*

"*Our purpose was simply to see whether or not she was connected. Obviously, she was. Finding out that she would consider leaving was an unexpected development.*

"*So we knew she was connected and very curious about the job. Even though I told her the search was not real, she set out on a crusade to find out which non-profit it was. Before too long, a few execs called Sheila to complain. Sheila brought her in for a conversation. Sheila told her that she knew about my actions and that I had made it clear that there was no real job. It was a question of confidentiality. If I had told her it was a confidential inquiry, why was she making phone calls? That was Sheila's focus.*

"*They met for an hour and pretty much spent the entire time discussing confidentiality. It did not go well. At the end, Sheila asked her about the rumors about her and Paul. Kate denied saying anything to anyone.*

"*Sheila said she was glad to hear it because there could be no compromise on the importance of confidentiality and that if she ever spread rumors or violated any employee's trust, she would be fired, for cause, with no further notice. And she wrote her up.*

"*It took no time at all. One nurse went to her to complain about her supervisor and, sure enough, inside of a minute, Kate called the supervisor, who called the nurse, who called Sheila, who called Kate. End of Kate."*

"I don't get it. Why did they put this in your lap?"

"Simple. I devised a plan to get rid of her just like I devise plans to promote services. First I had to do an analysis of our competition. Kate was the competition. I needed to know how much power she had. She had a lot.

"Next, I needed to know how to eliminate that power. That one was easy. What I did not tell you were the two questions that I asked each of the HR directors I spoke with. Question One was, 'Do you know anyone looking for a new opportunity?' No brainer. But Question Two was, 'What, in your opinion, is the most important quality for an HR director, especially one who will have to build a new department?' They all said, 'Confidentiality.'

"That's when I knew how to get rid of her. If she lost her job for violating confidentiality, no one would defend her. So Sheila made it clear that if she complained or badmouthed us in any way, we would tell the truth. And since it was all documented, Kate had no choice but to relent. When she was asked by her friends what happened, all she said was, 'It was time for a change.'"

"The first story will be easy to relate, but I don't have a clue how I'm going to explain 'Marketing Plan Kate' to my client. I'll probably do it over the phone!"

"May I make a suggestion?"

"Of course."

"Look, I'm technically senior management but in reality I come into the process at the end. I'm supposed to make things work.

"In this case, they had a problem. They had no idea how to solve it. So they came to me and I used my marketing

skills. First, and I know I'm repeating myself, I checked out the competition. If they had not called Kate I would have gone to her and asked her, in confidence, if she knew anyone looking for a job – just like I actually did. That was the second phase, planting the idea. You see with marketing it's all about getting people to think they want something that they don't realize they want. It's not all of marketing, but it's an important part. Salespeople will argue and say that that's sales, but I disagree. I consider it to be marketing. With marketing, I'm being proactive; when I was in sales, I was reactive. It was 'I have a solution to your problem.' Now it's, 'You don't know this, but you have a problem and I have a solution.'

"And one more thing; they trusted me. They could have gone to someone else but they chose me. I'm proud of that!"

"Nicely stated. And what I'll tell them, how I'll frame it, will be that when they had a purely managerial/supervisory issue, which required a great deal of sensitivity, they came to you for the solution and the implementation. That should go over well.

"Next question: if you could have any job, what would it be? It does not have to be realistic and the answer will not be held against you."

"It's stupid; you'll laugh."

"I've only gotten one stupid answer in all the years I have asked the question. And once you tell me yours, I'll tell you what it was."

"You have to understand, I have absolutely no relevant skills. I would probably destroy the planet. But I have always wanted to be a Nobel Prize-winning chemist."

"Not 'stupid' at all. In fact, it fits in with your marketing accomplishments. Identify a problem, find the solution, implement it.

"Now the 'stupid' answer, and I heard this from one woman and one man, was, 'I would love to be paid to stay home and watch my soaps.' Those were the only times I actually had to use the answer against someone. It became clear, after that point, that they were both very lazy.

"What is the largest number of individuals you have supervised at any one time?"

"Three."

"What's the largest expense budget you were ever responsible for – meaning you would have had to sign off on the expenditures, including salaries?"

"I'd have to approximate."

"It's not an audit; I'm just painting a picture."

"Let's say half a million."

"Have you ever been interviewed on television?"

"Numerous times."

"Radio?"

"Once or twice. Hated it. Don't know why, but I just didn't like it. Maybe it was the interviewers. They have to make up for the lack of body language by being boisterous. Not my cup of tea."

"Ever been interviewed by the press? Newspapers? Magazines? Trade journals?"

"More times than I can count."

"Do you write brochures? Newsletters? Press Releases? Annual Reports?"

"Yes. Yes. Yes. I've contributed to annual reports and proofread them."

"What about websites? Content, not the tech stuff."

"Yup."

"Do you have references? And I will want former supervisors."

"No problem, but not now."

"That's fine. I only check references when there is mutual interest in the position. And my clients understand that.

"But be prepared. Have a list of three past supervisors, names, contact info, how long and where you worked, and where they are now. Note if they are in a different time zone. Provide a one- or two-sentence summary about your relationship. It shows you are well organized and thinking about the needs of the person checking your references. And don't forget to call them. In fact, when you give the list ask them to wait until the next day to contact them so you can tell them to expect a call."

"OK.

"By the way, you haven't told me who your client is yet."

"You are correct. But let's just get some other questions out of the way. You see, I guarantee my clients confidentiality. So until I know that you are qualified, I can't tell you. But once I know, I'll tell you and then, and only then, and only with your permission, will I submit you."

"Fair enough."

"OK. Let's go down the list.

"Why do you want to leave your present job?"

"Like I said, I'm afraid I've marketed myself out of the position. I'm not sure what they are going to do, but the program is up and running and they don't need me."

"Why did you leave Tellescope? And, by the way, is it spelled with two 'l's?"

"Yes. Two 'l's. I loved it there. As you can see, I stayed for over four years. But they hired a new COO and we just did not get along. He actually provided me with a good reference which really shocked me."

"Remart Industries? And that's a non-profit?"

"Yup. And a good one at that. Employment opportunities for new immigrants while they learn English. Best job ever. Eight of the best years of my life. And the idiot founder used grant money to remodel his house. I could have killed him. I got a call from the press asking me about it. I was sick in bed. The reporter was a friend of mine. I told him he was crazy and I was going back to bed. The next thing I knew there was a knock on my door and I was being subpoenaed by the Attorney General. The SOB... Well, you get the picture."

"Under normal circumstances I would, at this point, remind you that it is an absolute 'no-no' to badmouth a former or present employer or colleague. However, in this case just sarcastically refer to him as 'the gentleman.'"

"Understood."

"The other jobs were so long ago no one is going to care.

"Let's review the job qualifications."

"'Master's in Marketing or a related field.' I think an MBA from Wharton is good enough."

"Thanks."

"'Minimum five to eight years experience.' You have well over ten. 'Non-profit and corporate.' Yup.

"And the rest is what I refer to as 'your mother loves you' stuff. Like someone is going to say they are not ethical, hardworking, and the rest of it. I never understand why employers include that nonsense in job descriptions. But anyways...

"Responsibilities. You have managed a team. You have been responsible for strategic planning. Have you ever designed and implemented a media campaign?"

"Yes. At Tellescope we launched a new product and I was responsible for the media. We had three five-minute segments on the local ABC and NBC affiliates, and Fox News Channel. I *got one radio interview and I arranged interviews for the CEO with the local dailies."*

"And what about budgetary supervisory experience? You already said you had been responsible for a half-million dollar budget, but did you prepare the budget and track it?"

"Track, yes; prepare, no."

"Don't worry about it, no candidate is ever perfect. And I let the client know anything that is missing so there are no surprises.

"And finally, do you have any experience with persons with special needs?"

"My best friend since kindergarten has Down's Syndrome."

"That's great!"

"What?"

"The client is Rosewood House. They provide services for the developmentally disabled. Have you ever heard of them?"

"I have and I even think that years ago I might have volunteered for an activity they were having. I went with Jimmy. But they wouldn't know me and I may have it wrong so don't mention it to them."

"What questions do you have for me?"

"I saw the salary range, do you know about the benefits?"

"They promised to send me the details. But for future reference, never ask what the salary range is. If they don't tell you, you should know. You're a professional and it's your profession. You should have enough information on the company to be able to guess the range. You won't know the benefits, but you will have a ball park idea of what a fair offer should be.

"So let's discuss salary negotiations for a second.

"First, don't be the first to raise the issue of salary. They'll know what you are earning. I'll tell them. So they know what they have to beat. Usually, I recommend asking for

a 10- to 15-percent increase, if it's local; 20- to 25-percent if the candidate has to relocate. But it depends on the responsibilities.

"Second, if they ask what you want, tell them. Tell them what you are earning and that it is not worth making a change for less than – and it's your call what you say. But add the caveat that it depends on benefits. Sometimes benefits are worth more than actual salary. Health insurance, pension, and days off can all translate to real money.

"And one last thing. Part of my services is to help with the negotiations. Don't tell them that you want to speak with me. That's inappropriate. I don't work for you, I work for them. But we all want to make this happen, so feel free to consult with me. In any case, they probably will ask me to get involved. And they will definitely give you at least a day to think over any offer. So don't feel pressured."

"Understood. What about their short- and long-term goals?"

"Don't know. All they told me was that the goal for this position is to market new programming. It's one of the frustrations of being a recruiter. Sometimes clients don't share everything with me. But these are exactly the types of questions you should ask them."

"Do you have any idea who I will be supervising and who will be supervising me?"

"Yes and no. You'll have four associates under you. I don't know anything about them except that the most senior has only been there a couple of years and that's why he was not chosen for the position. And, before you ask, the position is new. The COO has been supervising marketing, but they want to bring in a professional. And she'll be your supervisor. Her name is Helen Golding. Make certain you check her out on LinkedIn. And don't forget to go to Guidestar to review their 990. Knowing their website is not enough preparation for an *interview. You have to dig deeper. So make certain you do your homework.*

"Anything else?"

"No, I think you covered it all."

"Do I have your permission to submit your résumé?"

"Absolutely."

"Again, make certain to check them out. Not just the website. Google them. Dig deep. That will differentiate you from your competition. And they may have other candidates. Get the names of their key leadership. They'll be the ones interviewing you. Research them as well. You want to make a personal connection. That's the key to getting an offer.

"You are the first candidate I'm submitting. My process is to keep candidates informed of what is happening. When I hear from them you will hear from me. If you don't hear from me that means I have not heard from them. And it can take some time. They are a new client so I don't really know how long this may take. In any event, I nag on a fortnightly basis."

"Fortnightly? Do I detect Canada?"

"You do!"

"You're a big boy, so I won't have a problem calling you up and telling you that they are not interested or that they went with someone else. I do not leave my candidates hanging in the wind, or whatever the expression is."

"I appreciate that. In the past, recruiters I worked with..."

"Forgot about you the minute they didn't need you anymore and you never heard from them again."

"Correct."

"I don't work that way. You see I want this to be a long-term relationship. And I want you to refer your present and future employers to me when they are conducting searches. So why would I treat you like other recruiters?"

"Good to hear."

"Regardless of what happens, you are now in my system. So if something else comes up I will contact you. The important thing is, like I told you already, I advocate on your behalf. But for me to do that, you have to keep me in the loop. If you hear from them, and it happens all the time, make certain you inform me. Don't assume I know. And, like I said, when I hear from them, you'll hear from me."

"Sounds great!

"It's been a pleasure."

"All mine and I'll be in touch."

Sam's competition, Tony, had a similar interview. However, unlike Sam, his was a one-page résumé. He only had a few years' experience. It was good experience, but he just met the minimum requirements for the position. So this was age and maximum experience vs. youth and minimum experience.

They were both excellent candidates and I enthusiastically submitted both of them. Then things got interesting.

My client wanted to meet Sam. He was very impressed with Sam's résumé. It was seven pages of substance and he liked the idea of having someone who had worked, in one capacity or another, for some major players.

When Sam met with Robert, the HR manager, they did not hit it off. Robert didn't dislike him, but there was no spark. So it was Tony's turn and it was love at first sight. They really hit it off.

Rob set up a meeting for Tony with the COO and they too got along well. But the COO wanted to see Sam, just for comparison sake.

So while Rob was arranging for Sam to meet with his COO, I was checking Tony's references. All three were consulting clients. All three had known Tony for a good number of years and all spoke very highly of his work. The first was his brother-in-law, the second was the man who introduced him to his wife, and the third was his wife's best friend's husband!

Two things bothered me: the first was that Tony had not mentioned to me his relationship with his references. The second was that he had not bothered to tell his references not to mention the personal relationships to me.

When I sent my report to Rob he called me back laughing. He could not believe it. But it didn't matter. As I was checking references, Sam was meeting with the COO and they really hit it off. So I checked Sam's references. They were stellar. They described him as "brilliant." Sam got the job.

The funny thing is that this story is the perfect example of why attitude is so important. If you consider yourself to be "old" and feel you can't compete with the "young" guys, your negative attitude will cost you the job. If you consider yourself to be too "young" and can't compete with the "old" experienced candidates, that will hurt you as well.

Remember Alice? She never would have gotten the job – or any job for that matter. Her approach was to convince the interviewer why she was a bad candidate.

Sam and Tony had the right attitude. They convinced interviewers why they should be hired! They both had confidence and, in the end, as is always the case, it came down to personalities. Rob liked Tony more than Sam so he supported his candidacy – that is up until the time he showed himself to be immature. At that point, since the COO liked Sam more than Tony, Rob had no problem supporting him.

So there is no misunderstanding, if Tony had provided legitimate references, he would have gotten the job. As we learned in Chapter Two, attitude is everything. **But the lesson here is that it's not the length of a résumé that counts, but its quality – and having real references!**

CHAPTER FIVE:
Good Ole' Fashioned
Discrimination

BIGOTS AND RACISTS PROVIDE a good service. They give everyone a feeling of superiority. They are so unbelievably ignorant that they actually believe that what they are saying and doing are logical. So unless we are talking about circa 1930 Germans, it's doubtful that they will achieve anything but galvanize public opinion against them.

Trouble is, sometimes bigots and racists have enough brains to keep their big mouths shut. They do what they do without saying a word. But, not always.

I know of one recruiting firm who had a client who was the founder of her own non-profit. She was an elderly woman, probably in her 70s. It's no excuse, but culture can play a role. Permit me to digress.

There is a famous story about President Truman. Harry S Truman was a lot of things, but he was no anti-Semite. After he left office he granted an interview to a newspaper reporter who happened to be Jewish. He told him to meet him at his office, if I remember correctly, in the Court House in Independence, MO. The reporter arrived ahead of schedule and, after a few minutes, noticed the former president approaching, cane in hand, hat on head. On a human level, he saw an old man coming to a meeting with him, a young man, when he could have easily met him at his home. He said, and this is not a direct quote, "Mr. President. Thank you so much for agreeing to the interview. I appreciate it, but I would have been happy to have met you at your home. I feel bad that you came to me." Truman replied, "I live in my wife's mother's house. She never permitted persons of the Hebrew faith to enter." Truman was not being anti-Semitic, he was respecting his late mother-in-law.

I'll give you another example. In her autobiography, Agatha Christie recounts stories about how friends, who had lived in Africa, had had servants. She quotes them, her friends, as referring to them as "niggers." If she were writing today, she probably would have chosen to be more subtle. But for a Victorian woman writing in the 1950s and '60s (she started in 1950 and finished some 15 years later) she was merely reporting on events and dialogue as they happened. No political correctness and, no doubt on her part, no insult intended.

But to return to our 70-something non-profit founder...

An important question for a recruiter to ask a client is what type of person will succeed at their organization or company. Culture matters. It has to be a good fit. This does not mean gender or race; it means personality. People have to like their colleagues. They have to be comfortable with them. I am a neat-freak and very well organized. I hate clutter and mess. I worked at one place where the people were very nice, but issues of personal hygiene aside, their workspaces were never going to appear on the cover of *Good Housekeeping*. I stayed, but it was difficult.

The non-profit founder's answer to the question about the "type of person" was, more or less, "I wouldn't bother interviewing minorities. I have nothing against them. It's not for me you understand. They would not be comfortable here."

Given her age, it didn't surprise me when I heard the story. I have had older people, including one former colleague, when we first met, say "Some of my best friends are Jewish." And guess what, every last one of them was an anti-Semite. That's another thing I like about racists and bigots, for the most part, they can't help themselves. They don't know it, but they actually announce themselves loud and clear. All you have to do is listen...

But in any case, our issue is what to do when you believe you are being discriminated against.

John came to me as a career counseling client. He arrived on time, was dressed appropriately, greeted me with a firm handshake, thanked me for meeting him, and we got started.

"I have to apologize; I can't get my cell phone to shut off."

"The joys of modern technology. I've had the same problem with my phone. I took it back and they just took out the battery and put it right back in. I forget what they call it. Something like a 'soft reset.' It did the trick."

(He tried it and it worked.)

"Hopefully you are as good a counselor as you are a technician."

"Well you just proved to me that you are a good communications professional – or a least a good suck-up artist!"

"After 20 years, I better be!"

"So what are you doing here? You have had a good career. You have never left a job in less than five years. Each new job was an advancement. You also had at least one promotion at each of your jobs. Why make a change?"

"I'm tired."

"Bad answer in an interview. No one is going to hire someone who is 'tired'."

"Point taken. But that's not what I mean."

"I know. But I have found that it is not what you say that matters, it's what people hear. And if you say that you are 'tired,' they will hear that you are 'tired.'"

"Understood. Let's try again. It's time for a change. I've been working on the same type of projects for a long time. I want something new. New challenges. New opportunities."

"Good answer. So what have you been doing about making a change?"

"I've been applying for jobs I've seen posted on-line and in the papers. And I've been doing some networking. The problem with networking is that I don't want my boss to know I'm looking and the more I network the less confidentiality I have."

"You are absolutely correct. It's the perfect zero-sum game."

"And it might be hurting me. I've been looking for a good five-to-six months and have only gotten a couple of interviews."

"So what can I do for you? What will make you feel at the end of our session that your money and time were well spent?"

"May I be frank?"

"You have to be. It's the only way this will work. Some counselors will want to 'hook' you. They will want you coming back, over and over again, spending your money, making them rich while they slowly, very slowly, get you to draw the conclusions about yourself that they drew after 10 minutes. I don't work like that. I want you out of here in an hour or two, employed within weeks, and referring your friends to me.

"I can't achieve my goal if you are not brutally honest with me. And that's how I will be with you. If you're an idiot, I'm going to tell you you're an idiot. So, be frank."

"I think that I am being discriminated against."

"Any of them, or all of them?"

"Excuse me?"

"Well, let's see. To quote Don Rickles when he was roasting Sammy Davis, Jr. on the Dean Martin Show, 'You're black. I guessed!' You voted for Nixon..."

"McGovern, actually."

"So you are no spring chicken. I'm willing to bet that you are male. And, if I am not mistaken, you are wearing hearing aids."

"They're supposed to be invisible."

"I am all seeing and all knowing. I'm basically brilliant. And there is the little matter of the fact that when I came to greet you I thought I saw you repositioning one of them. I have had a couple of hearing impaired candidates and I noticed that you were basically making the same motion that they would make when the aid moved or was uncomfortable.

"So what is it? Race? Age? Gender? Disability?"

"I don't know. But it has to be something."

"OK. May I throw political correctness out the window just to emphasize what you are saying."

"OK."

"How many jobs have you applied for?"

"I don't know. 150-200."

"So, 175 employers don't want to hire an old, deaf, nigger with only one X chromosome?"

"I'm in shock. No one has called me a 'nigger' in years!"

"Feel free to call me a 'kike.' My intention was to shock – and you gave me permission. It's ridiculous. Maybe some

were discriminating, but all? No way. You are a pillar of diversification. If you were a veteran you'd be perfect."

"But I'm not getting any interviews."

"OK. We'll get to that. On your cover letter do you include information about age, race, gender or medical condition?"

"Of course not."

"So from the cover letter, all they know is your gender based on your first name."

"Right."

"I looked at your résumé. Guess what, I knew your gender, guessed your age, and was pretty sure that you were black."

"How did you know?"

"Once again I remind you that I am all knowing and all seeing. And it helps that you have a man's name, included your year of graduation from college, and that you have your photo on your LinkedIn profile."

"I bow to the master!"

"Why do you want to work for a moron?"

"Excuse me? I never said I wanted to work for a Mormon."

"Moron! Not Mormon. Since I called you a nigger, I'm going to have enough problems with the NAACP. Do you honestly believe I want the Mormons coming after me too?"

"Sorry. It's the hearing aid – or your Canadian accent."

"Explain."

"I was an English major. For a time I wanted to be a Henry Higgins. Despite the hearing aid I can still pick up an accent."

"I bow to the master!

"Ok so enough bowing. Do you want to work for a moron?"

"No."

"I thought not.   So if you are being discriminated against, you are being discriminated against by people for whom you would not want to work. So that means that they are saving you time and money by not calling you in for interviews for jobs that they have no intention of offering you."

"So I should thank them?"

"In a way, yes.   In any case, since you can't prove discrimination, let's try to find some other reason."

"It's your show."

"No. That's a serious point. It is NOT my show. It is YOUR show. You are responsible for your job search. No one else. No one can do this for you. This is YOUR show. I work for you. It's your show, but it is my process.

"Now, I asked you to bring with you some cover letters. Do you have them?"

"Yes, and I also brought the ads I responded to."

"Great. Now let's have a look.

"Donaldson Construction. Why did you apply there?"

"They said they needed someone with experience in the construction industry and I have that."

"Nope. Wrong. They said they 'prefer' someone with construction industry experience. They said they 'need' candidates with 'a Bachelor's degree in architecture or a related field.' You're an English major. You don't meet the minimum qualifications. That's why they didn't call you for an interview. You're unqualified."

"OK. What about Thompson? I meet all of their qualifications."

"No. Sorry, you don't. Read the ad?"

"'Thompson Enterprises seeks a seasoned communications director, with knowledge of the local business community...'"

"Excuse me. What was that you said? 'Knowledge of the local business community...?'"

"Yeah. So?"

"They are located in the Bronx. You live and work in Jersey. You ain't local and you don't know the local business community."

"But..."

"No 'buts.' Sorry. I worked in the Bronx for five years. I know, or knew, the Bronx. If you are not from the Bronx or in the Bronx you will never convince them that you know the Bronx.

"Next."

"This one I have all the qualifications for."

"Yes you do. This one you should have applied for. I like your cover letter. It's good. I see you told them what position you were applying for and where you found it. You even mentioned the date, which is three days before you e-mailed them. Guess what happened?"

"A million people sent in their résumés before me and they didn't even bother to look at mine?"

"I'd bet on it."

"Your problem isn't discrimination, it's process. You have competition. You have to beat the competition. You can do that with your qualifications. You're very good. But 'very good' is not always good enough. You have to focus on jobs for which you are qualified and get your applications in immediately."

"The thing is, I have a crazy schedule and sometimes it can take me days to research job openings."

"Describe your schedule."

"I get up about 5:30, do what comes naturally, workout for a good half hour, shower and by 6:30 I'm on my way to my girlfriend's. We have breakfast together and then I take her to

work, dropping her son off at school on the way. I come home around 8:00, leave the car, and get to the office around 8:30."

"Get to the office?"

"It's about a 10-minute walk from my house so, weather permitting, I walk."

"Why doesn't your girlfriend take her son to school and herself to work?"

"I enjoy it."

"Did you ever speak with her about the difficulties you are having finding a new job?"

"Sure. We talk all the time."

"Did you ever mention to her that you were having trouble with time management issues?"

"Nope."

"May I assume that at the end of the day you are too tired to do any job hunting?"

"That's a good assumption."

"Does your girlfriend respect you?"

"She loves me."

"Means nothing. I guarantee if you listen to her conversations with her girlfriends you'll hear that she loves shoes, some TV show, movie, actor, actress. 'Love' is the most overused and meaningless word in the human vocabulary.

"Does she RESPECT you?"

"I think so."

"Well, you have to find out. You have to explain to her that you do not have two hours to spend on her every morning."

"Two hours?"

"You leave the house around 6:30 and return around 8:00. That's an hour and a half. I assume you have a parking space at work and that your day actually can begin closer to 9:00 than 8:30?"

"So?"

"So at 6:30, instead of playing chauffeur, you sit down at your desk for two hours, sending out résumés. Around 8:30 you get in your car and drive to work. Instead of a 10-minute walk, you have a five-minute drive. You'll be in the office around the same time, and the only thing anyone will know is that you are no longer walking to work."

"They'll..."

"...ask you why. And you'll say, that instead of spending mornings with your girlfriend and her son, you're going to spend evenings. So you want the car at work so you can leave right away."

"But what if..."

"...she gets upset about having to drive to work and take her son to school? You explain it to her. If she respects you, she'll understand. If she doesn't, dump her. Why would you want to be involved with a woman who doesn't respect you? And this is not permanent. It's only until you get a new job. Or, it may be permanent if you will have a serious commute to work. In that case, you couldn't spend your mornings with her anyway, so better to find out now."

"You're tough."

"Yup. And in this case, I'm also right.

"You are not being discriminated against. You are applying either for the wrong jobs or too late for the right ones. Your cover letters are well written. Your résumé is excellent. I could suggest a few cosmetic changes, but they are insignificant. And you are clearly intelligent and articulate, so I have every confidence that you will interview well.

"Is there anything you haven't told me that could impact an employer's willingness to hire you? They will probably want to do a background check. Usually it's criminal, driving, and credit, and possibly a drug test. If there is anything negative *they could discover, you have to tell them before they ask you about it. Truth is, if they find something, and you haven't mentioned it to them, they probably won't even give you the chance to explain, they'll just move on to the next candidate."*

"No. A background check would be perfect. I have no health issues besides hearing. My credit is excellent. I've never been fired."

"Look. You know what you have to do. You need to find 10 more hours a week to work on your job search and I just found them for you. You are correct in going slow on networking. Confidentiality is very important. So just get to it."

To answer your question, she respected him. Once he had let go of fears of discrimination and started applying sensibly for positions, things turned around. He started to get interviews. There was a problem; he apparently was very nervous during interviews but did not realize it. (I certainly saw no evidence of it.) When he got home from an interview, he noticed that his shirt would be drenched with perspiration. It was summer, so he thought nothing of it. Then he realized that he spent most of his time in air-conditioned rooms or his car. He put two and two together and was worried that he was coming across as unsure of himself because of the way he was interviewing. We worked on it and eventually he got a job, ironically, close to his girlfriend's home. (In subsequent chapters I discuss interviewing in great detail.)

The lesson is this: Don't assume that if you are having a problem getting interviews it's the fault of the employers. Have someone review your process. To quote Shakespeare, "The fault, dear Brutus, is not in the stars but in ourselves."

PART TWO:
ACTION PLANS

NOW THAT WE HAVE dealt with the major problems people face with unemployment, real and imagined, self-inflicted and not, we are going to look at the actual ways different people, in different scenarios, have conducted their job searches.

CHAPTER SIX:
The High School Dropout

THE COMEDIAN RON WHITE has a show titled, *You can't fix stupid*. While I do not really appreciate his humor (it's a little bit too profane for my taste), he sure nailed the title.

I once trained an intern to work Reception. I told her, "When the phone rings, answer it right away, always before the third ring. Then say, 'Good morning. Thank you for calling XYZ. This is Mary. How can I help you?'"

She wrote it down. Nothing wrong with that. Some people like to have scripts. After a while, they throw them away.

That afternoon, I went to reception and heard her say, "Good morning. Thank you for calling XYZ. This is Mary. How can I help you?"

Now we are all human. We all make mistakes. I was standing there. She saw me. She must have been nervous. Right? Wrong.

"Mary, that was fine but you said 'Good morning.'"

"You told me to."

"But it's afternoon."

"You didn't tell me to say 'Good afternoon' in the afternoon."

You can't fix stupid and she was gone by the end of the week.

But you can fix foolish…

Some time ago I got a call from a woman who introduced herself as the mother of a thirty-year old Ph.D. in mathematics. She wanted to know if I could help him get a job. I asked what he was doing by way of a job search. She said that he was working at a "lab" (I decided not to question why a mathematician worked at a "lab"), and was always complaining about it. So she was taking the initiative and trying to find him a new job.

I asked her why anyone would want to hire someone who lacked the self-confidence and time management skills to conduct his own job search and needed his mother to do it for him. She replied, "He doesn't know I'm doing this."

I told her that the best thing she could do for him was to stop treating him like a baby. Then I told her to make a list of all the places she had sent his résumé and give it to him in public. She asked me why she should give him the list "in public." Without hesitation I said, "Since there will be witnesses, he probably won't kill you, even though, if you gave the employers his name, you've killed his chances of ever working for them. You made him a laughing stock."

She hung up. A week later her son called me. He thanked me profusely and told me that he had read his mother the Riot Act. His wife was pregnant with their first child. He told her that if she ever did anything like that again she would never be permitted to hold, play with, feed, change or be in the same room with her grandchild.

I then suggested that he go to his boss and tell him what happened. It was a good thing he did. Sure enough, his boss's counterpart at a competitor was a personal friend and asked him about the "mathematician whose mother is trying to get him a job." He was able to respond and turn the situation around.

But there was another situation I could not turn around...

Louis came to me about a year after dropping out of high school. His mother had called me asking for assistance. Unlike the previous parent, this one thought before she acted! She explained the situation to me, and I said I would be happy to meet with Louis if he was open to it. He was. I sent him my usual packet of questions and information, and he showed up for our session.

"Louis, welcome and have a seat."

"Thanks for meeting with me."

"My pleasure. Your mother seems to be more than a little worried about you. I saw your résumé. There's not much there. Why don't you just tell me about yourself."

"There's not much to tell. I'm 18. I dropped out of high school last year and have not been able to find a job. And those I find I can't keep."

"I saw that. But let's begin with the beginning. Why did you drop out of high school?"

"I hated the fucking teachers."

"Louis, in my office no one swears."

"Sorry. I hated the teachers. The classes were all boring."

"How were your grades?"

"Lousy. Are you kidding me? I was failing everything."

"Did you know that the unemployment rate for high school dropouts is roughly half again as high as that of high school graduates?"

"I don't understand."

"Let me show you. This is from the Department of Labor's website. That's the Federal government. In December, 13.8% of all high school dropouts 25 and older were unemployed. If they had stayed in school, only 8.7% would be unemployed. If they had some college or an associate's degree, it would have

dropped to 7.7%. But if they had stayed in school, went to college and gotten a Bachelor's degree, only 4.1% would have been unemployed. Those are real numbers."

"But I'm not 25 so what does it have to do with me."

"Everything. I don't have them but I guarantee you that the numbers for high school dropouts under 25 are even worse. Let me put it to you another way. With a college degree, the odds of your being employed are more than three times better than if you are a college dropout. What's more, over your lifetime, because you don't have a degree, you will earn over a million dollars less than someone with a degree.

"Do you understand?"

"Yes."

"Good. So this is your situation. You are uneducated, have no positive work experience, and I am willing to guess, because you have not been able to hold a job for more than a couple of months, you have attitude problems."

"The restaurant was not my fault."

"What happened?"

"We were told that it was OK to eat the food. When I would get hungry I would go in the kitchen and get something to eat. But the boss would get mad at me for not bussing the tables."

"When did you go and eat?"

"Around 12:00, 12:30."

"But that's the busy time for restaurants. That's when you were needed. That's why you were hired."

"But I was hungry."

"So were the customers."

"Yeah, but..."

"No. There is no 'but.' People go to a restaurant when they are hungry, not when you are full. You were wrong. And the fact that you lasted as long as you did shows that your boss

probably tried to help you."

"He said I could work in the kitchen, but I hated it. All I did was clean dishes."

"I think I am beginning to get the picture. Tell me something; what would your ideal job be?"

"I love fixing things."

"What type of things?"

"Clocks. Watches. Telescopes. Microscopes."

"Mechanical things. Not high tech."

"Right."

"Did you ever try to get a job with a jeweler?"

"Once, but he said..."

"...you needed a high school diploma?"

"No. He actually said he would teach me the business but he had a rule. He only hired people who passed background checks and drug tests."

"And which one were you worried about?"

"Both."

"Well, as I understand it, a juvenile record is not made public so it may not come up on a background check. You should ask an attorney. As for the drug test, stop using and clean out your system.

"Do you have a probation officer?"

"I had one."

"Did you get along with him? Does he like you?"

"I think so."

"So the way to deal with a juvenile criminal record, if it will appear on a background check, is for you to tell a potential employer that you were stupid, you did something stupid, got caught, learned your lesson, and now your probation officer is willing to be a reference. That way you show that you're honest.

"Here's the thing: If you tell something negative about yourself that they are going to find out anyway, then at least *they will give you the benefit of the doubt that you are to some degree honest. If you hide something from them, they'll assume you're dishonest."*

"That makes sense."

"Good. Now despite what the jeweler said, I doubt very much that you would ever get a serious apprenticeship without a high school diploma. You have to have one. Otherwise…

"Let me ask you something. Is there anything you would really like to own?"

"A Corvette."

"You and me both. Let's do some simple math: let's say it's a used Corvette and only costs $35,000."

"I found one for $30,000."

"OK. Thirty it is. Minimum wage in New York City is $7.25 an hour. But let's say, that by some miracle it goes up to $10 an hour. Most people work 40 hours a week. Let's say you work 60. That means every week you earn $600. That means that in 50 weeks you would have earned $30,000 to buy the car."

"Great!"

"Fifty weeks is a little less than a year. And, of course, you are not earning $600 a week. That's before taxes. You'll be earning a little less. And then there are the things you will need to buy: food, clothes, rent, to name a few. So let's say you save ten percent each week, $60. That means you'll have the $30,000 in 500 weeks, which is around nine and a half years. And that ignores the money you'll need for insurance, maintenance, and gas.

"See where I am going with this?"

"But I can't stand fuc… sorry… school!"

"You are not going to get a job, a decent job, where you can make a living and support yourself, without that piece of paper. You have to have a diploma. You are not alone. There are plenty of people who drop out of high school but they get an

equivalency degree. Look into it. Find out how and where. You really have no choice."

"My mother says she is going to kick me out of the house unless I get my act together. So I need a job."

"No, you don't. You need to get your act together. Get the diploma. Start studying. Make your mother proud and she won't kick you out. She doesn't want to kick you out. If she did, she wouldn't have sent you to me. She wants to help you by forcing you to help yourself."

"I guess so."

"I know so."

"What about your father?"

"Left when I was a baby."

"Can you go back to high school?"

"I think it's too late."

"OK. So find out about the equivalency degree. And as you are studying, go to jewelers and introduce yourself. The older they are, and the smaller the shop, the better. Be very polite. Dress very conservatively. Nothing wild. Put on a tie."

"A tie!"

"Yes, a tie. Most of these men are going to be east Europeans. I bet the jeweler you met with was wearing a tie, and if it was cool out, a sweater vest."

"How'd you know?"

"It's my job to know.

"Go to them and say that you want to be a watch maker and you want to learn the trade. Explain that you are studying for your high school equivalency diploma, don't expect to be paid anything, but would really appreciate the opportunity to learn about their profession.

"For the most part, they will be honored and it might appeal to their ego."

"What do you mean?"

"You'll be flattering them. And if they don't have any sons, or if their sons are not interested in the business, they'll sort of adopt you. It happens. And, of course, if they like you, once you graduate, they may offer you a job. Or, if they can't, they may help you find one. It's called 'networking.'

"At a minimum, you'll be learning a trade, getting your diploma and making your mother proud."

"And that's what I should do?"

"That's what you have to do. Because if you don't, you'll get yourself into real trouble. You have to clean up your act. No more trouble with the police, no more drugs, no more fooling around."

"Can I call you if I have any questions?"

"I'll be mad if you don't!"

I'd like to say this one turned out well. I can't. I don't know. I never heard from him again and his mother never returned my calls. **But the lesson is clear: Graduate from high school, graduate from college and, if necessary, clean up your act!**

CHAPTER SEVEN:
Everyone Has a Network

SOMETIMES MY JOB IS a lot of fun. A good example was when I met a truly nice person, with great potential, who was really smart and on her way to a great career. She just needed a little push in the right direction.

A recent graduate of City University of New York, she excelled in class, secured some internships, and came across as articulate and focused. Her problem: she couldn't find a job.

> *"Cindy, welcome! Have a seat."*
> *"Thanks for meeting with me."*
> *"My pleasure. So tell me, what can I do for you?*
> *"I'm doing something wrong and I don't know what it is. I just can't get a job."*
> *"First, what do you want to do?"*
> *"You saw on my résumé. I've got non-profit experience and I want to build on it."*
> *"Are you interviewing?"*
> *"I've had maybe an interview a month and it's been six months since I graduated. I live with my parents, and I really have to move out."*
> *"'Have to' or 'want to?'"*
> *"Want to."*
> *"OK. So first, unlike a lot of people in your situation, you are not on the verge of becoming homeless. You have a roof over your head, financial support if needed, and don't go to bed hungry."*
> *"True."*

"You might think that I am about to tell you that you are not alone in your frustrations about the job market. And you might also think that I am about to tell you that you can take comfort in the fact that your situation is expected and will not be held against you. But, sorry, I'm not going to tell you that.

"Let me explain to you my approach to finding a job. It all comes down to differentiation. You have to set yourself apart from the crowd. There are thousands, probably tens of thousands, of recent – and not so recent – college graduates looking for work around the country. That's an irrelevancy. I assume you are conducting a local job search..."

"I am. I can't relocate."

"OK. That's fine. So instead of tens of thousands of competitors, you only have to worry about the thousands in the metro area."

"Thanks a lot!"

"Give me a chance. I'm trying to make you feel better."

"OK."

"But it's not even thousands. It's probably tens or a couple of hundred at most. You see, you have a good education. You've got a Bachelor's from CUNY, which is a respected institution. You majored in Poli. Sci. which, as a graduate of a Department of International Relations I do not consider to be a true academic discipline..."

"What!?"

"You are sitting in that chair stiff as a board. You have barely moved your arms once. When we shook hands I noticed that your hand was cold. You are scared, nervous and tense. I am trying to inject a little levity into the situation and apparently failing miserably. So let's try this:

"BREATHE! RELAX! I'M HERE TO HELP!"

"It's just so gosh darn frustrating!"

"'Gosh darn?'"

"I don't swear."

"I'm beginning to like you. Now let me finish.

"You've got CUNY, Poli. Sci. – which is a fabulous degree to have! So you can smile! And, most importantly, you have minored in English. Question: Based on your education alone, what's going to differentiate you from your competition?"

"I have not got a clue."

"You speak English good and write even betterer!

"So you can laugh AND smile. Very good."

"English is going to save me?"

"Yup. You see most people, and I am sorry to say a large percentage of CUNY graduates who have sent me their résumés and cover letters are included in this, can't put a sentence together to save their lives."

"Well, we have a lot of non-native English-speaking students."

"Don't care. I got my degrees in Israel. When I arrived, I spoke no Hebrew. But I learned the language and had enough brains never to send a letter in Hebrew without asking a native Hebrew speaker to proofread it. The non-native English speakers should have had their letters proofread before they sent them to me.

"But that's not all. The English speakers were, in some cases, even worse. I have sympathy for the non-native English speakers. The English speakers would send me letters with Twitter short-cuts, or whatever you call them. One guy committed the cardinal sin of sending a letter in all lower case letters and no punctuation.

"There's no excuse for any of that. If your presentation is sloppy, that means your work is going to be sloppy. No one is going to hire a sloppy person. They are amateurs. Employers only hire professionals and, based on your résumé, you are already a professional."

"But I haven't done anything."

"Are you kidding me? This is your résumé, isn't it?"

"Yeah. But so what if I had a 4.0 GPA?"

"I'm not talking about the GPA. Personally, it's nice and all, but I could care less. You can be book smart and street dumb. How did you spend your summers?"

"It's on my résumé."

"I know, but I want to hear it from you."

"My first summer, I went to Italy and learned Italian. And the following two summers I had internships at non-profits."

"How did you get the second internship?"

"The exec of the first recommended me to the exec of the second."

"So let's see what will differentiate you from your competition:

"First, you have an excellent command of English. Second, you have international experience having, if I am reading this correctly, in two months become fluent in conversational Italian. Third, you have had two internships which provided you with real world experience. Fourth, you got your second internship based on a recommendation from the director of the previous year's internship.

"How did you get that first internship?"

"When I was in Italy, one of the girls in my class told me about this non-profit her father supported. She put me in touch with him and he got me the interview."

"And the fifth thing that differentiates you from your competition is that you already know that the best way to get a job is through networking.

"We'll get back to networking, but for now, do you know, statistically, what type of person gets the most second interviews?"

"What do you mean by 'second interviews?'"

"Call backs. You meet with an employer once and they invite you back for a second interview. It doesn't mean that these people actually get the most job offers, just the most second interviews."

"I have not got a clue."

"The reason I know that you are not networking is that you are very attractive. Attractive people get the most second interviews. It's not fair, but it's a fact. And in a lot of cases the employers are trying to convince themselves that they want these pretty people to work for them not because of their looks, but because they actually have something between their ears. In your case, you clearly do, so hiring you would not be because of your looks but because of your brains.

"If you were really networking to get jobs, you'd have call backs. My guess is that you are spending most of your efforts answering ads. Right?"

"Yeah."

"Now there is going to be one down side to hiring you. Something that concerns some bosses. Do you know what that is? It probably happened to you at both internships."

"The guys would hang around my desk."

"Bingo! You can have a cookie. And what did you do?"

"In the first job I told them I was busy and they got the hint. Last year the boss told them that if they didn't leave me alone he would fire them. They left me alone."

"Good boss. When you get a chance during an interview, tell the interviewer what you just told me. It shows that you take your work seriously, you're a professional, and want to be treated with respect. It should dispel any concerns."

"OK. But what does this have to do with networking?"

"I'm a member of the Manhattan Chamber of Commerce. In fact, I'm what they call an 'Ambassador.' Let's say I took you

to an event and introduced you to ten people. Now you have ten business cards. What do you do with them?"

"I send them all an e-mail and follow-up with a phone call."

"Nice. Wrong, but nice."

"Everybody does that. You have to do something different."

"What?"

"Go out and buy blank 'Thank You' cards. Nothing fancy. Immediately after you get home send a note to everyone. Write something like, 'It was a pleasure meeting you at yesterday's, date it the following day, event. I enjoyed our conversation and will definitely be in touch. All the best, and thank you for taking the time to speak with me' or 'for your advice.' In other words, the networking event was on a Monday, you mailed the letters Monday night so they went out Tuesday and arrived Wednesday. Just to be on the safe side, on Friday, after you have had time to do some research on the companies and individuals, you call all of them and ask for an appointment. They'll remember you, the note and they will agree. After all, you are showing them that you are professional, go the extra mile, and follow through. In your note you said you would call, and you did.

"And just as an aside, you would not really need me to take you to an event. You can do this all yourself. Go to the Chamber's website, become a member of Meetup.com, find free networking events and attend them. At Chamber events you will meet business people and non-profit pros who may be hiring. At other events, worst-case scenario, you'll meet no one who can help you but at least you'll be practicing your elevator pitch. Do you know what that is?"

"Yup. 'I'm a recent Poli Sci grad and I'm looking for my first real job, something that will let me build on my internships, international and non-profit experience.'"

"Almost perfect. Get rid of the first part. You don't want to emphasize youth and inexperience. Just say, 'I'm looking for an opportunity that will allow me to build on my internships, international and non-profit experience.' That will lead to them asking questions about all three. It's a conversation starter. That's what you want.

"Now let's discuss the appointment you'll have with the people you meet at networking events — or anywhere else, for that matter."

"OK."

"When you ask for the appointment, do not ask for a job. Just say that you enjoyed the conversation, are interested in learning more, and would appreciate it if they could spare ten or fifteen minutes to meet with you.

"They'll agree. You are, in fact, paying them a compliment. You are making them feel important and people like it when others make them feel important.

"You arrive a couple of minutes early. You shake hands, firmly, with a smile and immediately thank them for meeting with you. Let them take the lead. Some will ask you about yourself. Give short answers. Others will ask what they can do for you. All you say is, 'As I told you, I want to learn more about your business,' or 'profession,' whatever the case may be.

"Make certain you have done your research and know something about them. Since we are talking here about non-profits, go to Guidestar and check out their 990. Do you know what a 990 is?"

"Yes. It's their tax return."

"Correct. And just in case, if you are researching companies, you might want to try Hoovers, Broadlook, Zoominfo and LinkedIn, not to mention Google. Don't close any doors. I know you WANT a non-profit, but you NEED a job."

"*At a minimum, study their website and have some questions. Ask permission to take notes. They'll agree. On the top of the sheet have two or three questions already written down. You'll be nervous and might forget them.*"

"*Sort of like Rick Perry forgot what government agencies he was going to cut during that debate?*"

"*Yes, and never talk politics! Sooner or later, it will cost you.*"

"*No problem!*"

"*When you have reached the ten-minute mark in the interview, tell them that you don't want to impose and you already took up ten minutes. Say that you would like to stay in touch, and ask their permission to send them a list of non-profits or businesses you are thinking about applying to for jobs. Ask them if they would be good enough to review it. They will all agree and most will follow through. Don't bring it with you. You are building a relationship, so steps matter.*

"*When you get home, send a typed business letter thanking them for their time and the list of companies. Say that you know they are busy and will follow-up in a couple of weeks.*

"*Remember, you are not asking them to do your work for you. You are not asking them to call on your behalf. But if you can get them to agree to let you use their name, that's as good as their making the call. Sometimes, it's even better because they may forget.*

"*Now, in some cases, they'll get back to you right away. But in most, they'll forget all about you. Calling them in two weeks will remind them.*

"*Follow-up. Doing what you say you are going to do is key. You see, when you network, you are trying to turn strangers into advocates. You want them to recommend you to an employer looking to hire someone like you. They are only going to do that if they trust you, not with their PIN number, but with their reputation. If they say to a friend or business associate, 'Cindy's great. Call her.' They call you, leave a message, and you don't call them back, or if you meet and they ask for information and you don't follow through and get it to them, you make the person who set everything up, who arranged the connection, look like a fool and they will never help you again. What's more, they'll warn other people about you. You'll get a bad reputation. Understand?"*

"Understood. But what's this about a list?"

"You need to create a list, preferably on Excel, of the non-profits where you want to work. Include the organization's name, street address, phone number, website, mission statement, names of the CEO and HR director, e-mail addresses, and any openings that they have. Just about every company and non-profit lists opening on their websites. You don't want to apply for the same position twice. So you have to track everything you do.

"Just as an aside, there is another reason to track everything you're doing. It's an accomplishment. You'll see that in the first week you only contacted 50 employers, but after the second week you doubled your productivity in less time.

"Of course the downside is that you will become frustrated. You'll see that you have applied to hundreds of places and have only had a few interviews. But that's why you hired me. When you get frustrated, give me a call and I'll talk you through it.

"In any case, the goal of your networking is to get to the person responsible for actually making the decision to hire someone. What you are trying to do is to get that person to send you to HR. HR sending you to the decision maker is what normally happens. The 'abnormal' route is the quickest way to employment. Do you understand why?"

"*Because HR will figure that the decision maker wants you so the placement will be easy?*"

"*Exactly! So now tell me about the networking you have been doing?*"

"*Well, I have been studying karate since I was a kid. And I asked the sensei at my dojo if he knew of anyone looking to hire.*"

"*And has he been able to help?*"

"*No. Not really. He's a great teacher, but he believes in self-reliance.*"

"*That's the antithesis of networking.*"

"*I know. But that's not all I've been doing.*"

"*I'm listening.*"

"*I actually am on Meetup. I am a member of a number of groups.*"

"*Good for you.*"

"*Tell me about the members who show up at the events – I take it they are networking events?*"

"*Yeah. But I also belong to some karate and cooking groups.*"

"*Let's look at the networking events. Who shows up?*"

"*Well they are mainly people like me.*"

"*People who are looking for work, not looking to hire?*"

"*Yup. And now you are going to tell me that I am wasting my time.*"

"*Wrong! Let me repeat what I said a few minutes ago, but in a different way. These groups are important for the very reason that they do not matter one iota. The chances of your hearing about a job or getting a lead from anyone there are between slim and none. So if you make a fool out of yourself, it won't matter.*"

"*You said you like my elevator pitch. You know that these networking conversations don't last long. You move on to someone else. At the end I always ask them if they know anyone who is looking to hire, just in case."*

"That's OK, but most of these people can't help themselves, so the odds aren't good that they would be able to help you. It's possible, but I would not bank on it.

"Here's a different approach. If they knew of something, they would have told you without your asking. So you should not ask a stranger for help. Networking isn't exchanging business cards, it's building relationships. This person does not know you and you don't know them. Maybe you don't want them helping you. They may be losers and your being associated with them could hurt you."

"So what should I do?"

"Ask them how you might be able to help them. Then, if they return the favor and offer to help you, you know they may be a good resource. If they are just in it for themselves and not willing to reciprocate, you don't need them."

"What else?"

"You need to listen to how they react to your pitch. For example, when you say 'international experience' that's a good thing because, like I said, it's a conversation opener. 'What international experience?' If they don't ask then they clearly are not interested in you. Same for your reference about non-profits.

"And I apologize for bringing this up, but the guys might be engaging you in conversation for reasons other than employment-related matters. So if they are not asking you serious business-related questions, or if you find yourself in the center of five guys all trying to impress you and feigning interest in what you are saying, move to another part of the room. Find women to speak with or older men."

"How did you know that that happens?"

"Because I used to attend a lot of Meetup events. There was always that one woman who was constantly surrounded by the guys who were not looking for intellectual conversation. And she never had enough brains to realize what was going on. She liked being the center of attention for all the wrong reasons. And no serious person there, and I include myself amongst them, took her seriously. I don't want that to happen to you."

"Thank you."

"OK. So you go to Meetups for practice. And, by the way, don't just go to generic networking events. Attend, in your case, Meetups of non-profit professionals. You may actually get some good leads.

"In any case, the serious networking events are job fairs and business fairs. Let me explain the difference between them.

"A job or career fair is when businesses meet at a common venue in the hopes of finding candidates for positions they are looking to fill. The positions are almost always entry level...

"That's OK."

"...and very few people are actually hired. In fact, no one is hired at a job fair. It's more of a professional 'meet-and-greet' type thing. There are a lot of people, a lot of noise, and it's usually next to impossible to have a real conversation."

"So why go?"

"Because that's where the jobs are. Recruiters probably won't be able to help you because we don't get clients looking to fill entry-level positions. It's not cost effective. So job fairs are important.

"What you need to do is to hand out your résumé, collect business cards, make a good first impression, and follow-up literally the minute you get home. Send an e-mail, thank them for having spoken with you and for attending the fair (no one else will thank them for having been there!), attach another copy of your résumé and remind them of something that they said to you *when you met. Close by thanking them again, making it clear that you are interested in their company and in the position, and that you look forward to hearing from them.*

"If they handed you an application form, and you filled it out there, you should have asked them how you can follow-up. Specifically, when to contact them. If they give you a 'Don't call me, I'll call you' answer, that's fine. Just get the person's card and send them an appreciative e-mail like we just discussed, with the obvious difference being that you refer to the application.

"If they tell you to follow-up in a few days, or whatever, do it. In any case, send a thank you card and, where appropriate, mention that you'll be following up as per their suggestion.

"Clear?"

"Clear. What about business fairs? Why would I attend those?"

"They are a little better than the Meetups. The companies are not hiring, or at least the reps who will be there will not be hiring. So there will be less pressure on you. You can practice your pitch, but more importantly you are building your network. As with the hypothetical Chamber meeting, get cards and send each person a note thanking them for having spoken with you. Tell them that you would be interested in learning more about their company and call them in a few days."

"Anything else?"

"LinkedIn."

"I have a great profile and over 1,000 contacts."

"Very nice."

"How many do you have?"

"Over 30,000."

"THIRTY THOUSAND?"

"Yup. And they are the first people I turn to when I am conducting a search."

"So what should I do?"

"Send a message to everyone in your network telling them that you would appreciate it if they would keep you in mind if they hear of any openings in the metro area. You can send them in batches of 50. Just cut and paste and you should be done in an hour. If you have difficulties, I can show you how."

"No. I know."

"Also, in your profile, right under your name write, 'Seeking opportunities in non-profit program services' or something like that. That way, everyone who sees your profile, and make certain it is public, will know that you are on the market. It can't hurt. And make certain your profile photo is flattering and professional.

"And check the job boards in the different groups you belong to."

"I'm already doing that."

"Great!

"Now there's one other thing you might want to do when networking in the real world and with your LinkedIn contacts, if they respond to your message. Ask them if you can 'shadow' them."

"What in the world does that mean?"

"Tell them that you are interested in their work and wonder if it would be possible to spend a few hours with them to see what it is that they actually do. In this case you are playing on your youth and inexperience so, unlike with your 'elevator pitch,' that's what you lead with. And, of course, when you get a follow-up meeting after a networking event, you can also raise the issue of 'shadowing,' but use your judgment. You don't want to appear to be asking for too much. After all, you're asking them to review your list. It's your call.

"Continue to respond to ads. I'll give you my hand-out about how to write cover letters.

"Do you know what the most difficult thing will be to do?"

"What?"

"Being patient! There is no instant gratification in a job search.

"Now when you have an interview set up, call me. It's all included in the fee. We'll do a mock interview. When the real interview is over, I'll debrief you. And before you e-mail the thank you note to the employer, forward it to me to proofread. If you can't reach me, show it to your parents. It's critical that there be no errors and that it get out in a matter of hours."

"So when will I have a job?"

"Not as quickly as you want, and not as long as you fear!"

Every so often I am wrong. And with Cathy I was really wrong. She did get instant gratification...

Of all things, it was one of her karate classmates. They had a match against each other. Cathy kicked her and the woman fell just off the mat and hit her elbow. It was a freak accident. Cathy went with her to the hospital and stayed with her until her parents arrived. Her father was appreciative and offered her a ride home. (The girl's mother arrived separately and took her daughter home in her car.) On the way, he asked Cathy about herself and it turned out that he had a client in Italy. He saw this client as his way to expand his business in the EU. So he offered Cathy a marketing associate position at his company, with responsibility for European business development. Even though it was not a non-profit, she took it and, as far as I know, is still excelling.

The lesson? Never underestimate your network. A job offer might come to you when you least expect

it and from an equally unexpected source. And, never underestimate dumb luck.

CHAPTER EIGHT:
The Effective Cover Letter and Résumé

SOMETIMES YOU JUST HAVE to wonder. When Craig came to me he was stuck. He was a graduate of NYU. He had been working for three years at a PR firm that specialized in financial services agencies and, for obvious reasons, had been laid off. He was book smart and street smart, apparently had great references and a phenomenal network. But he just couldn't get an interview, let alone a job offer. He was Mr. Frustration when he arrived at my office, and deservedly so.

"Bruce, what the hell am I doing wrong? I can't figure it out?"

"On the phone we discussed the fact that your network is coming through for you. Did I understand correctly?"

"Absolutely. They make calls for me. I follow-up. I introduce myself. The person on the other line is very polite. And if I leave a message, I use the name of the friend who referred me and they always call me back. They ask for my résumé. I send it. They acknowledge and politely say they'll be in touch."

"Don't call me, I'll call you?"

"Yes."

"Any feedback from your network?"

"I'm the king of follow-up, and everyone knows I take criticism well. They all tell me that the response they get is basically that they don't have any openings right now. But I know in some cases that just isn't true. They advertise openings on their websites."

"You know the 'horse-zebra' advice to medical students?"

"Have not got a clue."

"When diagnosing an illness, the advice is, 'If you hear hoofs approaching, think horse not zebra.' In other words, don't over think the problem and don't look for a complicated explanation for what is or is not happening. Sometimes the simple answer, the obvious answer, is the right answer.

"I think the problem is your résumé or cover letter. Did you send a cover letter when you sent your résumé?"

"Of course."

"Let's do the letter first. Show me.

"This is what you sent?

"It's three pages long, single spaced. Who has time to read this?"

"It's too long?"

"Ya think?"

"But there's a lot they need to know."

"Let's see what you told them that they need to know:

"You were the president of a student group at NYU where you learned the importance of leadership.

"You were the R.A. for a professor who they may or may not have heard of.

"You are on the board of your church, where you have learned the importance of building coalitions.

"And after three pages of irrelevancies you thanked the guy for asking for your résumé?"

"Well this stuff is important."

"Let me tell you a story. It's true and was even written up in the Gulf News, *no doubt the leading newspaper in the U.A.E. Nice Jewish boy quoted in Dubai! Who'd have thunk it?*

"Here's what happened:

"I was working at a nursing home in the Bronx. We

were all required to take a cultural sensitivity training program. It was only a few hours over two or three days. Actually it wasn't bad.

"The facilitator put up signs in each corner of the room: 'Strongly Agree.' 'Agree.' 'Strongly Disagree.' 'Disagree.' Then she would make a definitive statement and have us go to the respective corner. Based on past experience, she knew the results ahead of time – more or less. Until she made the statement, 'Race does not matter in interpersonal relations.'

"When she said that, everyone went to the 'Strongly Agree' corner except for me. I went to the 'Strongly Disagree' corner. She was shocked.

"'You understand that you are saying that race matters and should be taken into account in interpersonal relations?'

"'Absolutely.'

"'How can you say that?'

"'Well, any other answer would mean that I'm a racist and a bigot. Saying race does not matter means' – and at this point I was just looking at the faces of the people standing in the opposite corner – 'there is no Hispanic history, there is no African American culture, Asian parents don't teach their children what it means to be Chinese, Japanese, Korean. And I have to say, on a personal level, that I find it highly insulting that you don't think that there are such things as Jewish morals, principles and values.'

"At this point everyone, except for one woman, came over to my corner. The next day she came to my office and was concerned that I thought she was an anti-Semite. I laughed. She explained to me what I already knew, that one of her parents was Hispanic and the other was black. They had brought her up believing that race does not matter. She could not understand anything else."

"Great story."

"Thanks. It's true and I'm very proud of it. Even the facilitator came over and congratulated me. Turned out they had been doing this program for years and it was the first time that anyone had said that race was important – let alone convinced almost everyone in the room that he was correct and they were wrong.

"So what do you think this has to do with your getting an interview?"

"I don't know."

"I'll tell you. Not a damn thing. It's totally irrelevant. It's just a story I like to tell. But it's not what you want to hear. And it's not what you need to hear except as an example of what NOT to do.

"You told employers a few things in this letter: you can't prioritize, you can't get to the point, you don't understand that they are busy. Why would they want to hire you?"

"But..."

"No 'buts.' Sorry. No one cares about any of this at this stage of the process. The purpose of the cover letter is not to get the interview. That's the purpose of the résumé. The purpose of the cover letter is to get the recipient to read your résumé. So let's rewrite the cover letter."

"OK. What do I take out?"

"Everything. Now move over here so you can see the computer monitor.

"You obviously know the format or structure of a business letter, so let's look at each paragraph:

"The first paragraph, since you are networking, is to thank the person for speaking with you and for asking for your résumé. You are dealing with people who may not open their own mail. If the secretary sees a résumé, she just might send it directly to HR. You want to make certain she shows it to her boss, so by reminding him that he asked for it, you're telling

her that he actually wants to see it. Then, mention the name of the person who originally referred you to him. Say that you have already thanked him for making the connection. Now the secretary knows for certain this is real.

"Just as an aside, if you are applying for a job you saw advertised, in the first paragraph state which position you are applying for and where you heard about it."

"Why is that important?"

"It tells the employer that you understand that it is important for him to know where he is getting the best return on his ad dollars. If everyone responds to the ad in the Post *and no on replies to the one in the* Times, *he knows where to advertise in the future.*

"Now here's the thing that everyone seems to forget: the job search is not about you. The job search is about the employer. You need him, he does not need you. He has plenty of people to choose from. So what you have to do is to focus on his needs, not yours. When you get an offer and begin negotiating, then the focus is on your needs. Until then, it's all about the employer."

"Makes sense."

"So, in the second paragraph you have to win him over. Give him the example of that one thing that you did, that one accomplishment, that sets you apart from everyone else. That's your problem. You haven't differentiated yourself. So, what have you done that no one else has done?"

"I'm not applying for jobs in financial services. I learned my lesson. So whatever I did was irrelevant."

"If that's true, you just threw away your work experience. Silly thing to do, isn't it?"

"OK. One of our clients was launching a new credit card. I was given the responsibility for the ad campaign. We were going to do it all in-house. Sometimes we would outsource, but the boss said we needed the money so I got the portfolio."

"Good for you."

"Not really. I thought the idea was stupid."

"To give you the assignment?"

"No. The new credit card."

"What they wanted to do was to give customers the option of paying an annual fee in exchange for a lucrative awards program or no fee and no program. I worked up a campaign around the theme of 'Choice.' It wasn't Apple's "Big Brother' commercial at Super Bowl Whatever, but we all thought it was pretty good – given the fact that the entire idea was stupid.

"Well, the bank reps came to the office and I made the presentation. I don't know why I did it, but in the end I said, 'This campaign will get you a lot of press from either the Pro-Life or the Pro-Choice community.' I meant it as a joke but it bombed. And when I say 'bombed,' I mean Hiroshima."

"I can see why."

"But then something weird happened. One of the bank VPs said that they had, I don't remember, ten cards. He asked the question, 'Why do we really need another one? After all, too much choice can be a bad thing.'

"He then told us the story of research done at restaurants. Those with long menus earned less than those with short menus. People, he explained, want choice but not to be inundated.

"So they dropped the campaign and my boss gave me credit for having killed it. He thought I had done so intentionally, but I hadn't."

"'While at RXK I successfully showed a client the possible ramifications for a new product line they were thinking of launching. As a result, they decided not to proceed. That is the kind of thinking that I will bring to...' That's your second paragraph."

"But it wasn't intentional."

"Who cares? You learned from the experience and now

could do it intentionally. And you yourself said your boss praised you. Will he be a reference for you?"

"Yes."

"Then he will probably tell the story. No problem. He'll back you up.

"Next paragraph: In this case it's referencing the attached résumé. If you are answering an ad, it should be a reply to any questions in the ad."

"That reminds me, what do I write if they want to know about salary?"

"Tell the truth. Just write, 'In my last position I was earning X, not including benefits.' You are not negotiating with them. All you are doing is answering their question. If you don't do it, they'll either reject you for playing games or for not being able to follow instructions. If you are applying for a job that is paying significantly less than what you had been earning, then just say something about being flexible given the economic times. It's not a great thing to write, because you are undercutting your negotiating stance, but if there's no choice, it probably won't be any worse than not saying anything.

"In any case, finish with saying that you appreciate his willingness to consider you and that you look forward to hearing from him.

"And that's all you need. Most people don't even spend ten seconds reading a cover letter. And this new cover letter can be read in less than ten seconds. A good cover letter needs to be short, sweet and to the point. All things being equal, it will get the recipient to read the résumé."

"I'm with you. So what about the résumé?"

"OK. Everything here is fine except for the opening. I commend you for not starting with an 'Objective' or 'Professional Statement;' both are meaningless. But you need to grab the recipient's attention. Just like people don't spend more

than ten seconds on a cover letter, they spend even less time on a résumé. That's why I always find it amazing that people spend the most time on the things that employers spend the least time on. Candidates spend days and weeks on cover letters, weeks and sometimes months on résumés, and practically no time at all on interview preparation. But anyways...

"What we need the résumé to do is to grab their attention. This is how recruiters and employers read résumés:

"First thing we do is to see where the person is located. If it is a local search, and they are out of commuting distance, that's the end of them.

"Second, we look at years of employment. If the candidate is a jumper, they're toast.

"Third, on the way down, literally as we are moving our eyes, we need something to stop us. So 'third,' if you will, becomes 'second.' That's why, right after your contact information you need to have a section, front and center, called 'Selected Accomplishments.' List five or six things you have done that set you apart from everyone else. It's all about differentiation. Use bullet points and the first one should be what you used in the second paragraph of your cover letter. That will get the recipient's attention.

"And fourth, we go to 'Education' to see if the candidate meets the minimal educational qualifications, and scan to see if the other qualifications are there.

"That's basically how it is done and why the 'Selected Accomplishments' section is so important.

"Any questions?"

"So what you are saying is that my problem is that I'm not grabbing their attention. I'm boring them with a cover letter and they never get to my résumé."

"Exactly."

"I'm not worried about your interviewing. You have not said a bad word about your former boss. Just remember, never end an answer on a negative."

"I don't follow."

"If you are asked, and you will be, about your weaknesses or about a bad supervisor, talk about how you overcame your weaknesses and what you learned from the bad supervisor. That way, you leave them with a positive feeling and not a negative one."

"Got ya."

"So, change the cover letter and résumé, and you should be good to go."

And he was. It took him a couple of months, but his network came through for him. He was invited by one of his networking buddies, Stephanie, who had been unemployed for a long time (and is the focus of Chapter Ten), to a family function. Craig was single and Stephanie wanted to set him up with Rachel, one of her friends. They hit it off and Craig made arrangements to pick her up at work the next day. Rachel introduced him to her boss and they had a private chat. The boss asked Craig for his résumé. He always had a copy with him. Steven, Rachel's boss, complimented him on the third bullet point in the Selected Accomplishments section of the résumé. That was all he read. He offered Craig a job on the spot. Rachel arrived and Craig and Steven parted company.

As Craig and Rachel were leaving to go on their date, he told her that he was going to 'dump' her because he knew it was never a good idea to date a coworker!

The lesson here is: It's not about you, it's about the employer. Make certain that your cover letter and

résumé grab his attention by highlighting what you can do for him.

CHAPTER NINE:
The Right Way to Interview

SOMETIMES YOU JUST HAVE to dig deeper. Dave was that sort of candidate. He should have had no problem at all getting a job. He was doing everything correctly. His cover letters were short, sweet and to the point, his résumé was engaging, he was networking in the right groups, he had no "baggage," and he was genuinely a nice guy. In his case, I had to become a detective.

"Dave, I just don't get it. I read your draft cover letter and went over your résumé with a fine tooth comb. I really have no substantive suggestions. Everything looks great. So what's the problem?"

"Pardon my French, but it beats the crap out of me."

"Tell me what you have been doing."

"I have a great network. My friends and associates have been getting me appointments."

"So you have been going on interviews?"

"About one every ten days."

"I've got career counseling clients who would kill for that many interviews."

"How many call-backs?"

"None."

"None? Out of how many?"

"All of them."

"No. I understand that. I meant, how many interviews have you had?"

"Sorry. I don't really know for certain. Probably around 25."

"OK. First, that is an unacceptable answer. You are

unemployed and therefore your full-time job now is getting a full-time job. Just like – and I am making an assumption here – you tracked what you did when you were employed – sales calls, meetings, follow-up, closes, follow-up after the close..."

"Absolutely."

"So why aren't you doing the same thing now? You need an Excel spreadsheet with the names of the companies where you have applied, the people who interviewed you, notes on what they asked, what you saw, what you overheard. You don't want to apply for the same job twice, and you don't want to forget something important when you get a second interview."

"I'll give you that one. And, before you ask, I always send a thank you e-mail after an interview, get them whatever they asked for and, don't bother telling me, I went to your website and read some of the articles you were quoted in. Now I also send a hand-written thank you note. I get the importance of differentiation."

"The people in your network who introduced you to the people who interviewed you, did you thank them as well?"

"Absolutely! I sent each one a bottle of wine."

"How many would have had the chance to hear back from the employer they sent you to?"

"Probably all of them."

"Let's make an assumption. Let's assume that your network referrers are hearing bad things about you from the interviewers. Would they tell you?"

"Maybe not?"

"Why not?"

"I don't take criticism well. I get defensive."

"Is there someone in your network who you are close enough to that you can call them right now and they'll share with you honest feedback?"

"Yes. Chris Mooney."

"It's kind of warm in here. I'm going to go get us both a cold glass of water. You call Chris and ask him if he heard back and what he heard."

"Will do. He should be in."

***

"What did he say?"

"He said that Jenkins, that's the guy he arranged for me to meet with, said I had a great résumé, perfect experience and a lousy attitude. He said that my answers to questions just did not ring true and that I was argumentative."

"Was that an accurate assessment?"

"No. I was providing clarifications."

"You may have thought that you were providing 'clarifications,' but they didn't hear 'clarifying,' they heard 'arguing.' And it's what they hear that matters. Whenever I give a class on working with the media, I always say, 'It's not what you say that counts, it's what people hear.' And I bet you can think of times someone said one thing to you and you heard something completely different."

"Wife accuses me of not listening to her."

"I hate to side with the wife, but she's probably right. And that's got to be our focus. So let's do a mock interview."

"Sounds like a plan."

"And in case I forget to tell you, make certain you call everyone in your network who got you an interview. Apologize to them. Tell them that you know you screwed up. Don't blame anyone or anything but yourself. Tell them you have taken a career counseling session and that you now know what you were doing wrong and it won't happen again.

"So now let me ask you a question. And when you answer it, answer it the way that you answered it when the employer asked it."

"How do you know what they asked?"

"With very few exceptions, they – we – all ask the same questions."

"OK. So what's the first question?

"Why do you want to work here?"

"Chris spoke very highly of you."

"Let's take this one question and answer at a time. How did you prepare for the interview?"

"I devoured their website. I knew the 'About' page by heart – including their mission and vision statements."

"Anything else?"

"I Googled them and discovered some press releases that had been issued."

"Very impressive. Anything else?"

"Nope."

"As a general rule of thumb, what you did was perfect, but you should also have Googled the people you were meeting with to find out if you shared anything in common. The idea is to make a personal connection with the interviewer. In the future, check out LinkedIn profiles as well."

"Sounds logical."

"Remind me. How did you respond when they asked you why you wanted to work at their company?"

"I told them that Chris spoke highly of them."

"So you really trust Chris, don't you?"

"He's never steered me wrong."

"Too bad you were driving and not Chris when you gave that answer."

"Excuse me?"

"You're excused but it's not going to get you the job. You probably gave the worst possible answer. You had done all of that research and yet, when you had a chance to show off your due diligence wizardry, you blew it. 'Chris speaks highly of you.' So maybe they should hire Chris!"

"Well, what should I have said?"

"That you share their mission or vision statement – and then, since you memorized it, recite it! Or you could have talked about being excited over what you read in one of the press releases."

"Oops!"

"Big time. Do you understand the difference?"

"Yes. So what should I have said when they asked me why I left my previous places of employment?"

"What did you say?"

"Look at my résumé. I've only had two jobs prior to my present one. The first one went out of business, the second was run by a crook."

"What did you say, exactly?"

"The first place was great, but they went out of business. We were a small fish in a very large bowl. The second was a disaster. The boss was a crook and I wanted out. I couldn't stand the guy."

"Good answer followed by terrible answer."

"I don't understand."

"The first place went out of business. You didn't say anything bad about the owner, about your boss. The place shut down. Simple. But then you broke the number one rule: NEVER say anything bad about your present or former employers. NEVER EVER. It's always toxic. The person who is interviewing you will figure that one day you'll speak ill of him, so why hire you?"

"So what should I have said."

"What I always say: 'I left for ethical reasons. I was very uncomfortable with some of their policies and procedures. Nothing criminal, you understand. But that's why I want to work for you. I see that you have a mission statement and if it's

*real and not just a bunch of words, that's what I'm looking for.'
See the difference?"*

*"Yeah. Nothing negative and you remind them that you
did your due diligence."*

"Exactly. But let's go back to due diligence.

*"An interview is a two-way street. You have the right
to ask questions and your questions have to prove that you did
your homework. You can't say, 'I'm a great researcher,' you
have to prove to them that you are and you do that by asking
insightful questions that you could only have come up with
based on research.*

*"So have a few questions ready. If you don't have any
questions, that means you are not interested in the job and they
will not make you an offer. Period.*

*"Now there are also a few standard questions to ask.
You can't very well ask them if it's a nice place to work. That
would be silly. But you can ask for the proof by asking about
the average tenure of employees, the turnover rate and if they
promote from within. The answers all speak to the question of
employee satisfaction. And that's something you need to know."*

"Understood."

*"What do you think the most important question is that
an employer will ask you?"*

"Why do I want to work for them?"

"Very good! You get a cookie!"

*"Were you ever asked a question and felt that the room
got cold after you gave your answer? In other words, everything
seemed to be going fine and then you gave an answer and the
person's body language changed?"*

*"Yes. As a matter of fact, that's what happened in my
last interview when they asked me about my weaknesses. And
before you ask, I said that I am a terrible procrastinator."*

"What floor were you on?"

"Excuse me?"

"What floor of the building were you on?"

"In the twenties. I don't remember exactly."

"So why didn't you just open the window and jump out. You committed 'interview suicide,' so why not go for the real thing?"

"Well what should I have said?   Everyone has weaknesses."

"You are correct. Everyone has weaknesses and, in fact, if you can't come up with any it's held against you. I already told you that it's not what you say that matters, it's what people hear. You told them that you procrastinate and what they heard was that you know you have a problem and don't do anything about it."

"But I do. I have tricks that I use to get over the procrastination."

"Did you tell them that?"

"No. I guess I didn't."

"What you should have said was, 'I've always been a terrible procrastinator. Or maybe I should say, an excellent procrastinator.' A little humor never hurts. Then continue, 'But like any other time I know I am at a deficit, I come up with ways to deal with it. I clearly organize my day around deadlines and I give myself rewards when I meet or beat a deadline. It's silly, but it works.'"

"I see the difference."

"Look, we could continue until dinner. The important thing is never to be negative including when talking about former and present bosses and about your weaknesses. Always end on a positive. You procrastinate BUT… Understand?"

"Loud and clear."

"Great. Now let me give you a few more pointers about interviewing.

"When you interview, you don't want to sound like you're bragging. So what I suggest is what I call the 'I vs. We' answer. At the beginning, say something like, 'Before I begin I want to make something clear. I have been lucky to work with great people. I realize that I have been part of a team. So when I say 'I' understand that I know that there is a 'We' behind that 'I.' But you are interviewing me, not the team, so I will focus on my contributions to the common efforts.'"

"Sounds good. Thanks."

"You're welcome. But there's more. I don't think you are doing this but, never sound desperate. It's unprofessional and no one is going to hire someone who behaves unprofessionally."

"OK."

"During the interview you have to relax. Think of the three 'C's: Be comfortable, confident and composed. If you organize your thoughts, you'll create the proper atmosphere."

"Great! What else?"

"At the end of the interview, express interest in the job. Most people don't do that. They ask about future steps, but never say that they are still interested.

"Also, a thank you e-mail is a great time, the perfect time, the only time for interview corrections and clarifications. A good thank you e-mail can save an interview. So if you forgot to say something, or could have said something better, use the thank you to rectify the situation."

"Thanks."

"Last thing: If you are applying for a full-time job and you sense some hesitation on the part of the employer to hire you, don't offer to do it part-time or on a contract basis. It can be tempting but don't do it. First, if they wanted part-time they would have advertised for part-time. And second, all jobs begin on a contract basis because all jobs start with a probationary period. So don't think about it and don't say it!"

"Thanks. I'll remember."

And he did. Later that week Dave had an interview. He kept everything positive. Showed off his due diligence skills and got invited back for a follow-up interview. When he was leaving, something amusing happened. Someone from HR went with him and followed him to his car. "Did you see the woman sitting in Reception?" "Yes." "She's your competition." "I don't stand a chance, do I?"

Well, it turned out that he did. He called me concerned about the exchange with the HR rep in the parking lot. I told him I thought he handled it perfectly. A little humor can go a long way. Apparently the HR rep thought so as well. Dave started work the following month.

The lesson: do your homework, show the interviewer that you know more about her and her company than she expects, never be negative, show confidence and express interest in the job.

CHAPTER TEN:
What to Do When You Are Unemployed

STEPHANIE WAS THE KIND of client I like best. She was referred to me by a satisfied client, Craig, who we met in Chapter Eight.

She had been unemployed for two years. She was a graduate of Cornell. She had ten solid years' experience in senior management. She had a phenomenal record of achievement. She had been with her first employer for three years and her second for seven. She wrote well. Her cover letter was perfect and her résumé was on the mark. So why couldn't she get a job?

"Stephanie, I noticed you didn't put 'matchmaker' on your résumé."

"Well I'm obviously not very good at it. Craig dumped her before the first date."

"But he did take her to dinner."

"Yes. And he made a point of telling the boss that since he was not starting until the following Monday, technically, they were not co-workers."

"I like Craig."

"Me too. Now do for me what you did for him."

"Technically, you did it, not me. You made the connection."

"True. But he pulled your revised résumé out of his pocket."

"OK. Let's split the credit."

"Agreed."

131

"*Now tell me what the problem is.*"

"*I can't get a job. I've been at it for two years. You saw my cover letter and résumé, and you know I network very well. I'm a great manager. This should be easy.*"

"*You're right. It should be. What's your approach to interviewing?*"

"*Short, concise answers. I talk in numbers. If they ask, I show graphs. Every claim I make is totally backed up by verifiable facts. I'm as good as I say I am.*"

"*How do you present the numbers?*"

"*I'll say something like, 'In my last seven years with H&H my worst year had only a 250% increase in revenue, and I have never taken on less than 3 new product lines in any fiscal year. We are talking tens of millions of dollars in increased revenue. I'm good at what I do but, understand, I recognize the fact that I have a great team. Great product development. Great product manufacture. Great customer service.'*"

"*Sounds perfect. You don't sound like you're bragging and you're recognizing that you are part of a team. I didn't hear anything wrong. So tell me, what do you say when they ask why you left H&H?*"

"*You don't know?*

"*H&H burned to the ground and the owners decided not to rebuild. It was a crazy day. First, the computers went down. Then we lost the phones. We couldn't figure out what was happening. They sent everyone home. One of the bosses complained that one of the women was wearing a strong perfume and he said that they should update the personnel handbook to forbid wearing perfume or cologne on the job. The other boss said that he smelled it too but that it smelled more like burning rubber.*

"*They put two and two together and came up with three. In other words, they thought that the computers and phones going down were somehow related to the rubber smell, so they called the Fire Department. Turned out, the fact that the computers and phones went down was totally coincidental. When the Fire Department arrived they felt around and found that one section of the floor in the warehouse was hot. The rest you can guess."*

"Terrible, but not problematic when looking for work. No one can possibly blame you.

"Let me look at your résumé again.

"What have you been doing for the last two years? There's nothing on the résumé."

"I have a strict routine. I'm up at 5:30 every morning. I respond to ads on a number of key employment sites and national newspapers. I want to get my résumé in first. When I'm finished, usually by 7:00, I workout for an hour, shower, have breakfast and then call contacts and make appointments. On a perfect day, I spend the afternoon with at least two decision makers and when I get home I send thank you notes. I stop my job search at 7:00 – unless I have a networking event – and relax. And I don't do anything on the weekends except answer Sunday classifieds."

"'Houston, I think we have a problem.'"

"What?"

"You've spent two years looking for a job. You have a two-year gap on your résumé. The reason you're unemployed isn't your fault. The reason why you are not doing what you are not doing is your fault."

"You lost me."

"You have not done anything for two years! Your competition has. My focus is always on differentiation. You are like the majority of people; you are focused like a laser beam on getting a job. And you are doing everything correctly. No problem with your cover letter, résumé, and I'm certain

interviewing. Except for one thing: You answer the question, 'What have you been doing for the past two years?' with 'Applying for jobs and networking.' Your competition replies, 'I can't sit around all day applying for jobs. I'd go crazy. So I answer ads early in the morning and in the evening, but I've taken some courses to learn new computer programs and to hone my skills. I've also done some charitable work as a volunteer and I've taken on a few short-term assignments just to keep fresh.' Who would you hire?"

"But I've got to get a job, and if I'm not applying for jobs, I'm not applying for jobs."

"It's not a zero-sum game. Making yourself a more attractive candidate IS part of your job search.

"From your rings I assume you're married?"

"Yes."

"Is your husband employed?"

"Yes SHE is."

"Any children?"

"No. You did hear what I said?"

"Yup. And since it's irrelevant, I chose to ignore it. And I assume you don't bring it up in an interview."

"I do."

"In the same way you did just now?"

"What do you mean? You made an assumption that I was married to a man."

"Yes I did, and so will 99% of people interviewing you. So don't make an issue out of it. No one is going to hire you for any reason other than your skills. They will not hire you, despite your skills, if you come across as someone with a chip on her shoulder.

"I have worked with many homosexuals..."

"We prefer 'gay and lesbian.'"

"I don't care. 'Gay' means 'happy and carefree.' I

consider it a demeaning term. I won't use it. I have submitted a number of homosexuals for positions with clients. Some have been hired, some have not. Just like anyone else. If you are qualified to do the job, that's all that matters. A very logical case can be made for hiring a homosexual. They can open up a market that is regularly overlooked. Your homosexuality is an irrelevancy unless you make it relevant. But showing attitude is the wrong way. Saying that you have good connections in the GLBT community is the right way. And if they ask you what that is, answer without evangelizing.

"Now can we get back to the important thing?"

"Yes."

"OK since you are married – notice I did not use air quotes..."

"I noticed. But you were thinking it."

"I was. Since you are married, I assume that you are not financially stressed."

"I get monthly alimony."

"Hang on. You were married, got divorced and are getting alimony?"

"Yes."

"But you told me that you are married. So why are you accepting alimony when you believe that you are presently married? Sounds hypocritical to me."

"We went to New York. Same sex marriage is not recognized in Jersey so technically I'm not married and he still has to pay alimony."

"When did you get married?"

"Three months ago. Why?"

"I guarantee you that your ex-husband will stop paying your alimony. He'll contend that since the marriage is recognized in New York as a marriage and not a civil union, that he should not have to pay alimony. He'll sue, make it public,

claim you are hypocrite, and put you in the center of a major public controversy. He'll make it look like your principles only go as far as your bank book."

"He wouldn't do that to me."

"Why not?"

"We're still friends."

"Friends don't pay alimony to friends. Does he know that you got married in New York?"

"Yes."

"Do you think that he told his friends about it?"

"Probably."

"What advice do you think they gave him?"

"To stop paying alimony."

"Right. And what do you think he will think you will do if he stops the payments?"

"Since we're friends, he'll probably think I'll do nothing."

"That's fine. And that may be what he thinks, but non-payment of alimony brings up a lot of legal issues – none of them pleasant. So he'll want a court order. And if you challenge it, you'll be the poster child for the anti-same-sex-marriage lobby in Jersey. Are you willing to accept that?"

"No. I couldn't deal with that."

"I didn't think so. And one more thing, I guarantee there will be a bunch of lawyers who will want to represent him pro bono. This case will go to the Supreme Court. It's a conflict between the laws of two States and the Court will ultimately have to decide it. It will be a landmark case and your name will become as famous or infamous as Dred Scott, Brown and Roe.

"You seem like a rational person; someone with a lot of common sense. The last thing you want is such horrible publicity. No one will touch you. And remember, I don't know your ex, but all men have egos. How do you think he feels knowing that his friends know that you dumped him for a woman?"

"I never said that I 'dumped' him."

"True. My word, not yours. But still, how do you think he feels."

"Humiliated."

"Correct. And part of him wants to humiliate you. So if you honestly believe that you are married, you have to do the right thing and have your attorney send his attorney a letter saying that you no longer are willing to accept any alimony. And return what he paid you over the past three months. Then it's a non-issue.

"You see, everyone has two Internet presences. The first one you control. It includes comments you have written on blogs, your LinkedIn profile, your personal website, Facebook, Twitter, whatever. The other is outside your control. It's what other people say about you. Who's going to support you? The homosexual community will be furious for your making them look foolish, and everyone else will think of you as a hypocrite. You can't win.

"Now do you see why it is important not to bring any of this up? You have given me two reasons not to hire you: you have a huge chip on your shoulder when it comes to your homosexuality, and you are a hypocrite."

"I take exception to that."

"Don't. I guarantee you that every employer who interviews you will think the same thing if you bring any of this up. Now tell me the truth, have you?"

"No."

"There is no chance that you have a reputation in your industry for being an extreme homosexual and a hypocrite?"

"None whatsoever and I resent..."

"Good. I want you to resent it and, more importantly, to remember it. And you'll notice I have not questioned your honesty. You know as well as I do that lying in an interview is

stupid, and lying on a résumé can get you fired for cause. Which is my segue back to your résumé.

"We need to add a new section, sub-section really, under 'Work Experience.'"

"But I have not done any work."

"You're going to. Let's call it 'Recent Employment-Related Activities – 2009-Present.'"

"And what will we place there?"

"Everything. We just have to see what you have actually been doing that we can list and decide on what you are going to start doing."

"I'm listening."

"OK. You're on LinkedIn, correct?"

"Yes."

"I'm always getting invitations to take part in webinars. Have you watched any webinars since H&H?"

"Yes. A new version of the sales software we used to use came out and the sales rep invited me to watch a webinar on the updates."

"Great. That's the first one.

"Have you taken any courses?"

"Are you acquainted with the Learning Annex?"

"As a matter of fact, I am. I've done a few classes for them."

"I took two classes. One on speed reading and the other on getting a book published."

"Two more. Now tell me about this book."

"I've been writing a novel about a saleswoman. It's sort of a mystery romance."

"Is this real or just a pipe-dream?"

"It's real. I'm almost done."

"Do you have a publisher?"

"No. I've sent selected chapters to agents. I'm hoping to close with an agent this week."

"So why doesn't any of this appear on your résumé?"

"It's not relevant."

"Of course it is. If I say anything that is remotely inaccurate stop me."

"OK."

"When H&H burned down, it was an opportunity for you. You had been working on a novel and now you had the chance to actually write it. So you did what you always do when you have a new product to promote. You researched it. In this case that meant taking a course on getting published. And you networked with agents. Now you are about to close with an agent and to finish the first draft of the manuscript."

"OK."

"So why in the name of Susan B. Anthony have you not presented yourself that way?"

"I'm an idiot."

"I never insult a client – or argue with one!

"But I'm still not satisfied. Except for the whole marriage thing, which Craig never told me about and which is why I actually believe it's not a big deal as long as you don't make it one, you have not caused any red lights to go off in my head. But something isn't right. You don't seem like the type of person who could actually be content for two years just applying for jobs. Like the book, is there anything else you have been doing that you think is irrelevant?"

"I helped my pastor with a church fundraiser."

"I'm tempted towards violence! Why would you not think that is relevant?"

"It was just a volunteer project."

"Your pastor, did SHE appreciate it?"

"HE did."

"And did he think that it was important?"

"Yes."

"So add it to the list. We now have a webinar, two courses, author and volunteer. What exactly did you do?"

"We have elaborate, 19th-century wood carvings throughout the main sanctuary. We needed to have them cleaned. It's a difficult process that can only be done by a few companies. It's amazing the amount of gunk that accumulates over the decades. We never really noticed it until one of the windows was broken. The repairmen mentioned it. I created the campaign for the fundraising effort."

"How much did you raise?"

"The goal was $150,000. We raised $225,000."

"I swear I'm going to hit you!

"Don't you think that would be impressive to an employer? Why wouldn't you mention it?"

"It's not work!"

"Who cares? Did you research the people who were interviewing you?"

"No."

"Why not? Didn't you research potential clients before you met with them?"

"Of course."

"So what's the difference?"

"Point taken."

"So you research the people and you discover that one of them is a board member, or what have you, of their church. And you say, in passing, 'You might appreciate this since you are involved with your church...' He'll then ask you how you know and you'll be able to reply by saying that you always research the people you'll be meeting with. Call it 'due diligence.' And then you continue with the story."

"I guess I really blew it."

"Look. You can't change the past. But now that we have updated your résumé, and you have the right answers to the obvious questions, you should be alright."

And she was. On a personal level, she called her attorney and told him to see to it that the alimony was cancelled. Her ex was pleasantly surprised and admitted to her that he was thinking about going to court. Stephanie saved herself a world of hurt by doing the right thing.

Maybe it was karma, but once she ended the alimony, and refunded the past payments, things started to turn around for her. She signed with an agent, which meant that she could honestly say to an employer that her book was under consideration and they would then take her claim of being an author seriously.

She also started to get serious interviews. Surprisingly, the interviews came from responding to ads, not networking. When she landed a job it was a senior managerial position. The employer did not care about what she had done since she had lost her job; all he cared about was what she had done for H&H. But he did like the idea, and commented to her about it, that she had kept busy and tried to improve herself. Ironically, he did raise one concern. He included in her contract that she would be forbidden to write any stories, fictitious or factual, about her work for him and that when her book is published it had to be stated clearly that it is based on her experiences prior to joining his company. First amendment issues aside, she agreed.

The lesson for our purposes is this: you can't stay home and be idle when looking for a job. You have to be productive and grow professionally. You have to

view unemployment as an opportunity. That's what employers want to read on a résumé and hear in an interview.

PART THREE:
Failing and Succeeding

SO FAR WE HAVE looked at finding a job, applying for a job and interviewing. But the interactions have all been with me, a career counselor and executive recruiter. Clearly, employers are different. So, if I will be forgiven a certain amount of repetition, in the following two chapters we will consider, based on after-interview reports from my clients and candidates, the case of one of my clients who blew it, and one who was perfect.

CHAPTER ELEVEN:
Sometimes You Just
Have to Wonder

THIS WAS NOT MY search. Well it was. I was responsible for it. But figuratively speaking, just as you can say "It's not my day," this was not my search.

I found the perfect candidate. As a matter of fact, I had found four perfect candidates. A couple of weeks after I submitted them and they were interviewed, two accepted offers elsewhere. Even though I had asked them if they were under serious consideration for other jobs, they did not bother to tell me about their status with those employers. The third withdrew her candidacy because of a death in the family.

That left Doris. Doris was great. Perfect résumé. Perfect interviewing skills. Perfect personality for the client. In case you have not figured it out yet, employers hire people they like. I knew they would like Doris, and they did.

And then it happened...

The client called and asked me to check references. A sure sign that they wanted to hire her. Doris provided three professional references. I immediately started calling them. She had prepared a list that not only gave me the names of her references and contact information, but a little blurb about each one. Perfect; just what I would expect from a professional.

I called the first reference and it was glowing. Could not have been better. I immediately started typing up my notes to share with the client and then an e-mail arrived.

Doris had copied me on her thank you letter to the client. As soon as I read it, I stopped checking references.

Sure enough, the phone rang. It was my client. "Did you see the letter?" "Yup." "We can't hire her." "I know. I'll keep looking."

Her letter was full of spelling and grammatical errors. It was shocking. In person she was the consummate professional. In writing, she came across as an amateur. Guess what. No one hires amateurs.

Ironically, thank you letters can save a bad interview. If the candidate neglected to say something, or misspoke, a well-worded thank you letter can save the situation. But, as with Doris' case, it can also destroy a candidacy and cost a job offer.

If that was not bad enough, I quickly found a replacement for Doris. We met in my office. I saw her; she saw me. We went through the entire process. She was Doris #2. A perfect candidate. It only took about ten days from the time I met her to the time that the client told me to check references. They were great – and her thank you had been proofread. Then it happened again...

I called her to make the offer – which would have meant a $25,000 increase for her – and she said, "By the way. Would you mind telling them that I'm Orthodox and can't work Friday nights and Saturdays?" I wanted to kill her. I was livid. She made me look like a fool. I dreaded the call. But first I let her have it:

"Didn't you read their website?"

"Of course I did."

"And didn't you notice that the programs you would be responsible for run on Fridays and weekends?"

"Yes, but I thought they have to make accommodations for religious persons."

"No, they have to make reasonable accommodations
– REASONABLE!   It is not reasonable to expect an
employer to change their programs to suit a new hire."

The client was very nice – nicer than I was! And,
sure enough, I found yet another candidate. You can
already guess. Perfect on paper, great interview with me,
they really wanted to meet her. Only took a matter of days
to arrange the interview. And then Helen arrived.

She met with Margaret, the owner. Her HR director
was out sick so this would be the best type of situation: a
first interview with the actual decision maker. No filter.

Helen arrived on time. She wore no perfume and
only a little makeup. She was dressed conservatively.
She shook hands with the receptionist. In fact, when
Margaret asked the receptionist what she thought of her,
she remarked that Helen was the only candidate who
ever shook hands with her and, even more importantly,
engaged her in a substantive conversation about the
company and why she likes working there. Perfect.

(I recently confirmed my view about the importance
of shaking hands with, and engaging, the receptionist
while attending a Manhattan Chamber of Commerce event
at Microsoft's offices in mid-town Manhattan. I asked
the receptionist what percentage of visitors shook hands
with her and engaged her in conversation. She said, "six
percent." I then asked her if it would bother her if people
shook hands and spoke with her, assuming that she was
not busy. "Not all all," she replied, "I'd enjoy it.")

When Helen met Margaret she immediately gave
her a firm handshake and thanked her for inviting her in
for an interview. At the end of the interview she thanked
her again. When she got home she sent a thank you e-mail,
no typos, and mailed her a hand-written thank you card.

Everything was perfect ... except for the fact that by the time the card arrived I had already told her she was out of the running.

An executive recruiter works for the employer, not the candidate. I report to the client, the employer, what the candidate tells me. I might word things a bit differently, but I never lie nor distort. I'm proud of that and my clients appreciate it. When I asked Helen why she left her last job this is what she told me:

"My assistant used my signature stamp to write herself some checks. When she got caught, she said that I told her it was alright. She made it seem like I had approved loans for her, advances on her salary.

"Of course, I had done no such thing. I pointed out that the first check had been written three months earlier and she had not repaid it. So there was no evidence of any loan relationship. And I said the idea was preposterous.

"The problem was, it was a she said-she said situation. My boss said that he believed me, but advised that there was no way of knowing what the owners would decide. I could be fired. So he suggested that I take early retirement, my record would be clean, and that would be the end of it. He also promised to provide a glowing reference – which he has. And I was promised that my assistant would be fired by the end of the month. She was."

These things happen all the time. I believed her. Her story was credible and she had indicated that I could call her boss to confirm. I did. He did. They told the same story. I chose to believe her.

In the interview with Margaret this is what Helen said:

"I hired a young woman as my assistant. She was like a daughter to me. When she got into a fight with her boyfriend, she came and slept on my couch because she was afraid he would show up at her apartment.

"Then one day Finance came to me and asked me about some checks I had written to her. Nothing surprising about that, I did it all the time. I'd give her a petty cash check, in her name, she'd cash it, bring back the money and then we'd submit the receipts. You know how it works.

"Well, for those checks there were no receipts. And 'Petty Cash' was not written on the memo line. There were five checks, dating back three months, for around $1,000 dollars. Since Finance does things on a quarterly basis, they were only now discovering them.

"I immediately called her into my office. She burst into tears. Begged me not to report her and said she would return all the money by the end of the week. She also said that she would resign.

"She explained to me that she needed the money because her mother had some bills and a collection agency was harassing her. She pleaded with me not to report her.

"I told her that I had no choice. That I had to. She had committed a felony and I could not hide it. But, I told her, it would be better if she went to the boss and confessed.

"She agreed. She went right into his office and told him that I had given her some loans and that she was having problems paying them back. She wanted to work out a payment plan with him.

"Loans are not permissible. And, of course, I never did it. So when he called me in, I told him the full story. He said it was going to be a she said-she said situation and, that since I was eligible for early retirement, I should take it. If the owners

thought I had given her loans I would be fired and would lose my
pension. So I took it and learned from the experience."

Two things here:

First, "I learned from the experience..." is the perfect
way to deal with a negative. Most people will forgive you
your literal and figurative crimes as long as you explain
what you learned from the experience. So that part of the
answer was the right thing for Helen to say.

But, second, she gave a completely different answer
to Margaret. If she had kept to the basic facts as she had
related them to me, everything would have been fine. But
she painted a different picture for Margaret than she had
painted for me. All of a sudden there was a boyfriend,
a mother, bills, a collection agency. She lost credibility.
And she lost a job offer.

This is similar to what happened with another
candidate. The client called me, "Bruce. She's just what
we are looking for. Great job! Just one thing. She didn't
stop talking. We could not get a word in edgewise. She
made the interview a monologue, not a dialogue. We
need you to find another one just like her, but someone
who doesn't talk so much!"

For the record, I did. I found someone who didn't
talk as much and, more importantly, I found someone
who Margaret hired.

The lesson here, you may be surprised to hear, is
not simply less is more, don't talk too much, and don't
change or embellish your answers. The lesson is what
happened between me and my client. Even though I
had a string of bad luck with the candidates I submitted,
Margaret didn't fire me. She could have. But she didn't.
I was always honest with her and reported fully to her

about the candidates and their references. She trusted me. And that's the main lesson of this chapter. Be honest!

CHAPTER TWELVE:
The Art of Listening

PHILLIP WAS THE FIRST candidate who let me do something that I had wanted to do for years – place a for-profit professional in a non-profit.

My client was the Greshon Foundation. It was founded in 1980 by the Greshon family in memory of their son/grandson David, who was killed when he was hit by a bullet while playing in his backyard. There were no witnesses and the perpetrator was never found. It was assumed that it was a freak accident but, for obvious and understandable reasons, the family launched a campaign to restrict the purchase and ownership of firearms.

Personally, I have no problem with gun ownership. The only thing I would demand is that persons who purchase guns have to take a course, pass a test, get a license, take out insurance, and purchase a safe container (cabinet, trunk, whatever) to store the weapon and ammunition. When I served in the Israeli Army, I was told that when I went home, the M16 was to be placed on top of the highest piece of furniture in my home, and the magazine with the bullets had to be somewhere else. Why? Because I was responsible for anything that was done with my weapon. If someone had broken into my apartment and stolen the rifle, and the bullets, it would have been my head – almost literally! That's my philosophy. If you buy a gun, it's your responsibility. You misuse it or lose it, whatever happens with it is your fault.

The Greshons did not agree with me. They wanted a ban on all weapons. When we met, they asked me my opinion. I told them the truth. I think they appreciated my honesty because I got the contract. They wanted me to find them a director of Communications.

Needless to say, if I have a career counseling client, like Phillip, who is qualified to work for one of my recruiting clients, I like to make the match. It's a perfect world. What could be better? Someone comes to me for help getting a job, pays me for my advice, and a few months later I actually get him a job with one of my clients. What's not to love?

The problem was, Phillip was not qualified. He had no non-profit experience. Non-profits – wrongly and foolishly – are hesitant to hire persons who lack a non-profit background. Even though they have all of the skills and all of the experience, and even if they have the right education, non-profits still don't want them. "They won't understand us," they tell me. Or, "We're mission based. He'll be focused too much on the bottom line." Like that's a bad thing.

Usually, I don't even try to get them to change their minds. It's futile. This is especially true if the search for candidates goes quickly. If, in a couple of weeks, I am able to submit qualified candidates, and the client likes them, then that's it. I've done my job.

With Greshon there was a problem. Too many cooks in the kitchen. The number one problem I have with clients is that they do not have their process in place for hiring. It takes too long and they lose the best candidates. That's what happened. I submitted three stellar candidates. How do I know they were "stellar?" Simple. Within a month they all had new jobs.

Those three were great candidates. They kept me in the loop. I kept on reporting to Greshon that they were all interviewing. Finally Greshon set a day aside to meet with all three, one after the other. Four family members met with each candidate for almost two hours. They said they would get back in touch. I reminded them that they had competition. Two weeks later, one day after the other, I informed Greshon that all of the candidates had accepted positions elsewhere. "I'll renew the search," I told them.

At this point, after I finished an aggressive workout, I remembered Phillip. I called him up. He still had not found work. I sent him the job description. The first thing he said to me was that he was not qualified. I told him not to worry about it, that that was my problem. I asked him if he was interested in the job. He was, so I brought him back for another interview.

We decided that the best way to market him would be as a top-flight Communications director, an excellent communicator, with a business background who would be able to help Greshon with their process issues and get their message out. He agreed.

Since I was submitting an out-of-the-box, meaning unqualified, candidate, I called my contact at Greshon and explained to her that since they had lost the best non-profit candidates, now I wanted them to consider one for-profit candidate. I played a bit on their conscience. They knew I had worked hard in putting together the initial panel of candidates. They also knew I was upset with them for having procrastinated and having lost all of them. In a word, they owed me. So they agreed to interview Phillip.

Like John, who we met in Chapter Five, Phillip's problem was that he was a nervous interviewer. The way not to be nervous is to convince yourself that you have nothing to be nervous about. There will still be some nervousness, but it will be manageable.

On occasion, guests on my radio show, *Bruce Hurwitz Presents,* will confide in me that they are nervous. I immediately tell them that they have nothing to be nervous about. First, the vast majority of people who listen, listen because of the guest, not because of me. So if they do not spread the word about the interview, few people will know about it. Second, I control the interview. So if someone calls in and asks a rude question or makes a rude comment, I'll cut them off and put them in their place. But most importantly, third, I can always delete the show. If the guest does not like it, it will disappear, never to be spoken of again.

For the record, all of that is true. However, I don't remind them that I promote all shows to my network of over 30,000 individuals. And I also don't remind them of the fact that close to 6,000 people have listened to my shows. They know it. That's how I convinced them to be interviewed in the first place. But nerves set in and facts are forgotten. As long as they don't think they have anything to lose – after all, I told them I'd delete the show – why be nervous?

So with that philosophy I assured Phillip that he did not have a snowball's chance of getting the job. I told him to use it as a good interviewing experience. I told him that one of the Greshons was a trial attorney and he would ask tough questions. But I also told him that he was a very nice person, with a great sense of humor. Out of all the interviewers, the candidates I had submitted all remarked that they most enjoyed interacting with him.

Phillip arrived 10 minutes early for his interview. He had researched the Foundation and all the family members. He had been a catcher on his college baseball team, as had Sally Greshon on her college softball team.

The grandfather had written a review on Amazon about a book Phillip had also read, *Team of Rivals*, which was about Lincoln's cabinet. He was prepared to make the personal connection that is so critical in getting a job.

After the normal pleasantries, Richard Greshon, the grandfather and Board chair, began the interview.

"Why should we hire you? You have no non-profit experience."

"I know communications. You have a communications problem. You need someone who can promote your cause. You're not selling widgets, you're selling an ideal. You have a personal story to tell that is becoming all too common. Children are being killed, it seems about every week, by stray bullets. People are getting used to it. The story doesn't resonate like it used to. It should, but it doesn't. The same old non-profit approach to communications just will not work anymore. You need something new. You need a new perspective. That is what I have to offer."

"Give me an idea of what you are thinking."

(This is a dangerous question. If you come up with a substantive answer and they don't like it, your goose is cooked. You also don't want to sound presumptuous. Phillip gave a perfect answer.)

"It would be presumptuous of me to tell you how to promote your foundation. Even though I have studied your website inside out and backwards, and dug deep, I still don't KNOW you. Big deal, so Sally and I are both former catchers. I know what it takes to be a successful catcher. Does that mean anything? Not really. Only that we share something in common. And that's the key to successful communications.

"Think of your reaction, Sally, when I mentioned being a catcher. You looked up from reading my résumé. You were surprised. That's how I market. Right now I'm marketing myself. You are all my target customers and I'm the product I'm trying to get you to buy.

"Now even though I have gotten Sally's attention does not mean it's a good thing. She might be freaked out, think that I'm stalking her. For the record, I'm not. I just do my homework about my target audiences.

"Your target audience is everyone. That might actually be a problem. Let me freak all of you out and especially you, Richard.

"I would consider a campaign with the NRA. Yes, you heard me right, the NRA. And if anyone argues with me you will have to deal first and foremost with your grandfather because he supports me."

"This should be good!"

"Your grandfather wrote a review of Team of Rivals *on Amazon. One of the points that he made was that the genius of Lincoln was that he worked with his rivals, his opponents. He did not see them as enemies. Most anti-gun groups view the NRA as an enemy. What if you were to view them as 'the loyal opposition?'"*

"You have my attention."

"He has OUR attention," Sally corrected.

"The NRA does not want children shot. Why not sit down with them and work together on a piece of legislation to keep children safe? If they refuse, you go public and they look like monsters. If they agree, everybody looks reasonable. You take the initiative, you get the credit."

"And the blame," Richard added.

"True. But I looked at your 990. It appears to me that your funding comes from the family, not the general public.

What do you care if people are going to be angry with you? They don't financially support you. You have nothing to lose. And if reporters ask, all you need say is, 'We are willing to do whatever it takes to protect children. If others don't like it, that's their problem. We'd rather save one child's life by working with the NRA than the alternative.'"

Richard called and told me that it was the first time he could remember his family members being speechless! They did not know how to respond. They both hated and loved the idea at the same time. But what they all appreciated was the different approach to that of the normal non-profit professional.

Mark, the attorney, was next to chime in. He asked all the usual questions: Why did you leave your previous positions? Why do you want to work for us? What are your strengths? What are your weaknesses? What type of compensation are you looking for?

I had reiterated to Phillip the importance of giving brief answers. As we have already seen, when you tell the truth, but talk too much, you raise doubts. And sometimes you just talk yourself out of a job. Phillip had no problems in this regard. He gave perfect answers: Professional growth. No room for growth. The company closed. All true. All simple. All totally logical.

But the key, of course, was the negotiations phase. When Mark asked him about compensation, Phillip responded, "I was last earning $115,000." Then, as per my instructions, because I knew he was high for them, he added, "but it all depends on the benefits and the challenges. As I said, I am looking for new challenges. If I am confident I will have job satisfaction and a feeling of contributing to something important, the dollars will take care of themselves."

And they did. They offered him $95,000 with full healthcare benefits for him and his wife. Vacation days, sick days, and personal days were similar to what he had. The one thing that bothered him was the pension. He would not be vested in their plan for a year, so he asked for an additional $5,000 which he would invest in the pension, pre-tax dollars, with no match. It was reasonable, they agreed, and the deal was done. Negotiating about needs, not wants, being logical and unemotional, is almost a guaranteed negotiating strategy.

This is what usually happens. You can make one counteroffer, but it has to be based on needs, not wants, and be documentable. I had another candidate who rejected a $10,000 increase in salary because his commute to the new job would cost him $5,000 in gas and tolls. He documented it, made it clear that a move for a net increase of $5,000 was not worth it, and my client raised the offer $5,000.

This would be a good place to discuss how to resign. If Phillip had still been employed, once they handed him a signed offer, he would have written a resignation letter and handed it to his boss. Since he had had four weeks annual vacation, he would have given four weeks notice. In his letter of resignation, he would have thanked his boss for the opportunity to work for him and listed some of the projects that he had worked on of which he was especially proud. This would have been important because it is impossible to know what an employer will put in someone's personnel file. This way, he would have countered any negatives with a list of positives.

If his boss surprised him by making a counteroffer, I would have told Phillip that it was always wrong to accept a counteroffer. You see, if you accept a counteroffer you have destroyed your reputation with the new employer, and let your present employer know (a) that you are not happy and (b) that you'll do anything for money. In the back of his mind, he'll think that you'll look for another job just to get more out of him. In the long run, it never works.

The lesson here is, listen to what the interviewer is asking. Phillip picked up on their concerns. He didn't preach. He provided them with food for thought, not a real answer to their question. He let them know how he thought, what his process was. That's what they bought into, the process, not necessarily the proposal.

PART FOUR:
GRADS AND VETS

FINALLY, TO CONCLUDE I want to look at two distinct groups, both of which are having a very tough time in this economy: recent college graduates and discharged veterans.

CHAPTER THIRTEEN:
Fresh Out of College

DAVE CAME TO ME a week after he graduated from Fordham...a nice Jewish boy with a degree from a very good Catholic school. But unlike Cindy, who we met in Chapter Seven, Dave did not have any internships. His résumé was rather unique.

> "Dave, come on in. Congratulations on your graduation."
>
> "Thanks. It's weird. This is the first time in my life that I don't have a school to go to come fall."
>
> "I know the feeling. I had the same one when I completed my Master's and was waiting to enter the Israeli Army. It's sort of like something is missing from your life."
>
> "Exactly."
>
> "But what fills it is a job. And that's why you are here, isn't it?"
>
> "Of course."
>
> "I see that you read the articles and material that I sent you and you set up your résumé following my model. Thanks."
>
> "Well, it would have been silly not to. Why should I come to you for help and then not take your advice?"
>
> "I'm prejudiced, but I have to say I like your attitude!"
>
> "Format aside, what do you think about the substance?"
>
> "Let's actually look at both.
>
> "First, you have listed both your cell and e-mail address. The cell is fine as long as the voice-mail message is professional."
>
> "It is."
>
> "And you are using your Fordham e-mail. Will you be able to keep it?"

"I think so."

"Double check, just to be on the safe side. If there is any doubt, get a Gmail account, but make certain you have a serious address. Use your name, initials, numbers, no silliness."

"Understood."

"The margins are correct. Looks like half-an-inch top and one-inch bottom on the first page, and one inch all around on the second page. And you are using a 12-point font."

"Yup."

Your 'Selected Accomplishments' are all university related. I don't like that. We'll work on it.

"'Employment' is non-existent. Certainly you had some jobs?"

"I've never worked for anyone. Never received a paycheck. My focus has been on volunteering. I've been a volunteer since I was 12."

"OK. That makes you unique. I've never had anyone who has never had a job, but I have also never had a client who has been a volunteer since he was 12. So that's your first bullet point under 'Selected Accomplishments,' 'Dedicated volunteer since the age of 12.'"

"Employers will care about that?"

"First, let's be honest, it's all we've got. But it's a lot. Non-profits will love it. And it shows that you are 'mission focused.' All good!

"Now, under 'Volunteerism' you only list names, no details, so we have to make each, or rather format each, as though it was a job. But let's finish with the other things.

"Where's 'Languages and Skills?'"

"I knew I forgot something. I have a good knowledge of Spanish and no special skills. I'm a whiz with Microsoft Office."

"So we add Spanish and you might as well put Office; can't hurt!"

"OK."

"Let's get back to 'Volunteerism,' which I want to change to 'Community Service.'*

"Tell me about Central Valley Hospital."

"When I was 12, my best friend was in a stupid accident. He broke both his legs. He was in a hospital room with three other kids. Their parents visited but all they did was depress the kids. Parents worry; kids want to play. So when I was there I created crazy games. We had a lot of fun. Even the parents joined in."

"What kind of games?"

"Well, the kids weren't ambulatory – a word I did not know at the time! – so they were word or number games. The first kid would name an animal. The next would name one that began with the last letter of the previous word. So 'dog' would be followed by 'giraffe.' But that one got old quick."

"Did you know that in nursing homes they use similar games to help the Alzheimer's residents?"

"Actually, I did. One of the nurses told me."

"So what were the other games?"

"Reciting the alphabet backwards was fun. When the head nurse was not around, we would see who could keep an inflated surgical glove in the air the longest. And before you ask, she was worried that they would miss the glove and hit one of the machines. She was right! It actually happened but no damage was done."

"So how did you become a volunteer?"

"Jake, that's my friend, his doctor noticed that morale in Jake's room was higher than the other rooms. He mentioned it to one of the nurses who told him about my visits – I came every day after school to see him, give him his homework, and get back the previous day's. Doctor Mike came in one day when I was there, watched for a few minutes and then said he wanted to

speak with me. I was certain he was going to kick me out, but he complimented me and asked me if I would like to volunteer.

"I'm embarrassed to say, but I was not sure what he meant. Needless to say, he explained it and I became the Pediatric Ward's 'Chief Volunteer.' HR even gave me a badge with the title. Every year they would change the photo, but I would not let them change the title. I was, and still am, very proud of it, even though it was obviously given to me because I was just a kid."

"Yes. But it was also recognition."

"And that's why I would not let them change it."

"OK. So your next bullet point is 'Invited to be Pediatric Ward volunteer and remained so for six years.'

"This is how we'll write it up:

"'Central Valley Hospital – Pediatric Ward Volunteer – 2002-2008 – Responsible for creating and supervising interactive activities for patients.'"

"They weren't all 'interactive.'"

"'...interactive and individualized activities for patients.'"

"Great. So now you will want to know about the Historical Club."

"Good guess."

"I love history. You saw that that was my major. As soon as I arrived at Fordham I went looking for a volunteer opportunity. I went over to the Historical Club and asked if they had anything. The receptionist told me they were full but I could fill out an application.

"I sat down, filled it out on the spot and handed it to the man who happened to be the executive director. I didn't know that, and it was probably a good thing because if I had, I would not have done what I did."

"What did you do?"

"I'm a Civil War buff. They had a display which I looked at before I spoke to the woman at Reception. I spotted an error. I told the executive director that the sign said that the Gettysburg Address was 262 words long. There is some debate over the exact wording but clearly they were referring to the 272-word version. That's what I told him."

"And what did he say?"

"That I should report to his office first thing Monday morning with a schedule that would not interfere with my studies, and that I would be a volunteer fact checker."

"Your turn. Write it up."

"'Historical Club – Volunteer Fact Checker – 2008-2012. Responsible for fact checking all Club publications and displays.'"

"Good job. One question: Why didn't you volunteer at a local hospital?"

"I had had enough. When I got older they let me spend time with the terminal pediatric patients. It was too much for me. I became very friendly with one of the girls and when she died it was really hard. Doctor Mike asked me if I wanted to be a physician or a nurse. I told him I didn't. He said that if I had said that I did, he would have yelled at me and made me continue with the terminal patients. But since I did not want a medical career, he let me off the hook."

"Do you understand why?"

"I didn't at first, but a new doctor, a woman, took it just as hard as I had when she lost her first patient. He yelled at her that maybe she should try another profession and that if she wanted to be a doctor she should get used to losing. He told her to get out of his office and to only come back if she wanted to be a doctor.

"Everyone heard and the staff all knew what was going to happen. She came out, cried at the nurses' station and then *a minute later he came out, slammed a patient's chart on the counter and told her to get back to work.*

"She picked it up, walked away, opened it and all that was in it was a piece of paper saying, 'When I lost my first patient, I cried longer than you did and my supervisor yelled at me louder than I did at you. If you hadn't cried you wouldn't be the good doctor I know you are. Now go wash your face and start becoming the great doctor I know you can be.'"

"Doctor Mike must have been one hell of a doctor."

"He still is."

"OK. So now we have the résumé and the 'Accomplishments.' And keep two or three of the original ones from Fordham.

"Now the tough question: What do you want to be when you grow up?"

"An historian."

"Not a big demand, but not impossible. The exec at the Historical Club, can he help you network?"

"Yes, and he is."

"Good. But I was wrong about your résumé. We have to add a few things to 'Skills.' How do 'Detail oriented' and 'Empathetic to persons coping with illness' sound?"

"I don't like 'empathetic.' It sounds like other people are rude. How about: 'Knowledgeable regarding proper interactions with persons who are ill and their caregivers?"

"Excellent.

"Now let's think about a practical job. Let's try the obvious, a Volunteer Department in a nursing home."

"People die in nursing homes."

"When I worked at a nursing home, it was about a third of all residents each year. But the difference is, they lived their lives and their suffering ended. It's a lot different than with kids."

"You sure?"

"Nope. It may be just as bad for you. We are all different. Sometimes, if I was close to the resident, it bothered me more. But my attitude was that their pain was over. Nothing to cry about. But then again, I'm a tough S.O.B."

"I don't know."

"That's why you interview for jobs...see if you like them. And if it's not a match, in this case because of not being able to cope with death, it is not going to hurt your future employment opportunities if you say, when asked, 'I couldn't take it.' Nothing to be ashamed of. And, with your permission, I'll even call my contact at the nursing home where I used to work."

"But I want to be an historian."

"Who said you can't be an historian? I'm just trying to help you find a job. If you want to be an historian, you need a Ph.D."

"I know. Well, don't 'need' but 'should have' is more correct. But I want a break from school."

"So what's the problem? You get a job working with volunteers, and apply to graduate school. In three years' time, you have three years' employment, a Master's, and can go on to work as a fact checker for a publishing house, a radio or television station, or a website. All places where you might even want to look now."

"I didn't think of those. I've been focusing on newspapers, magazines and journals."

"That's logical, but don't dismiss the idea of working in a Volunteer Department. I'll be happy to make the call. At least, let me arrange an interview with my former colleague. She's the director of Volunteer Services at the nursing home. She's very nice, will invite you to lunch at the cafeteria – the food is unbelievable; I gained 20 pounds when I worked there – and *she'll tell you about the joys of being a Volunteer Department professional. Can't hurt."*

"What will you tell her?"

"That you came to me for career counseling. You have a wealth of volunteer experience, including at a hospital. You're looking for your first job out of college. I thought you guys should talk."

"That's it?"

"If she has an opening, or knows of one, she'll tell you. Bring a copy of your résumé, but don't hand it to her unless she asks for it. And she will. And don't ask her for a job or if she knows of anything. Like I said, she'll tell you.

"After the meeting, send her a thank-you note and ask her to keep you in mind. Remember, as far as she knows, you just want to learn about working in a Volunteer Department. Immediately saying you want to, well, that won't sound too good. So put it in writing, telling her that you have thought about it, and if she knows of anything you would be grateful for her help."

"What about the historian positions?"

"That's why God invented Google. Get to searching, then start applying. And, in any case, send your résumé to the HR departments of the local radio and TV stations and networks. Let them know you are interested in a fact-checking position. And send me the letters before you send them out so I can check them. It's all included in the price."

"I can't thank you enough. So you'll call your friend?"

"As soon as you leave."

And I did, and she offered him a job on the spot, took him for lunch, introduced him to other volunteers and, totally by accident, introduced him to a resident who was a Civil War buff. That closed the deal.

When he contacted me to tell me about it, I told him to still send out his résumé for the fact-checking jobs. A small radio station, that had a weekend history show, offered him a contract assignment fact checking for the program. He had the best of both worlds.

The lessons: All experiences are important, take advantage of opportunities and don't be afraid to spread your net wide.

CHAPTER FOURTEEN:
Fresh Out of the Corps

THE MISSION OF MY company is to promote the hiring of veterans. I do that in two ways, by lowering my executive recruiting fees by one-third when a veteran is hired, and by offering free career counseling services to veterans. I take my relationship with veterans seriously; not that I don't my relationship with non-veterans. Don't misunderstand, everyone is treated equally, but when I am able to help a veteran, well, let's just say it feels special.

Jeff came to me straight out of the Corps. He had served in the Marines for six years, and was granted a medical discharge. He was a Gunny, meaning a Gunnery Sergeant. A commander of men and women. A leader. Short hair cut. Strong as an ox. Over six feet, and around 225 pounds. Big guy. Formidable. "Takes possession of a room," as they say. A handshake like a vise grip. With a stare that could melt the side of a tank. And one of the sweetest guys I have ever met.

"Have a seat. Do I call you 'Jeff' or 'Gunny?'"

"I prefer 'Gunny,' but I think I need to get used to 'Jeff.'"

"You're right. You do. And there is something else you have to get used to."

"What's that?"

"Shaking hands with civilians. The idea is to relate purpose and conviction. The idea is not to break bones!"

"Sorry, Sir."

"And that brings me to the next issue. No 'Siring' and absolutely no 'Ma'aming.' With men, calling them 'Sir' just

seems out of place. Too formal. With women it's different. I have heard stories of veterans not getting jobs because they called the interviewer 'Ma'am.' Before you say it, I know, it's stupid, but it's life."

"There is a lot of stuff I am going to have to get used to."

"Yes, and the first is making a résumé. You said you have never had one and don't know what to do."

"I don't have a clue. I went to your website and read some of the articles, but I'm not a writer, I'm a decision maker and implementer. I'm a team builder."

"Sounds like the start of a résumé to me!

"But first, tell me about yourself."

"I ran away from home when I was 17. Enlisted on my eighteenth birthday. I had always wanted to be a Marine. My family life was horrible. From what I had read about the Corps, seen on television and movies, it seemed like the Corps would provide structure and be a surrogate family. That's what I wanted."

"So you have never had a job? Did you graduate high school?"

"Yes Sir."

"Bruce."

"Sorry, Bruce, I should have been clearer. I ran away after I graduated high school. I wasn't going to leave until I had the diploma. I may have been young and foolish, but I wasn't stupid.

"And, no, I never had a job. I did a few things before I went into the Corps – stocking shelves at a supermarket, delivering packages, things like that – for a few months. That's all."

"OK. You enlisted, went into the Corps and were obviously successful. You told me that you were given a medical discharge. What happened?"

"We were on the range. One of my sergeants was showing a private how to remove a bullet from his weapon. He did not realize that he was standing on a loose piece of ground. When he put his weight on his back foot, he lost his balance and the weapon discharged. It was a fluke. He could not have done it intentionally, but somehow he shot me in the knee. We were – are – the closest of friends. No one could believe it. I couldn't. He couldn't. But it ended my career."

"First thing, the way you tell the story is perfect. You did not use any military jargon – and I know you could have."

"Let me tell you something. The one thing I had to learn in the Corps is how to communicate. So I have learned to speak to civilians as thought they were 12-year-olds. Not talking down, mind you, but keeping things simple and not scary."

"That's crucial to finding a job, or rather, getting hired. You have to speak 'civilian.' It's the biggest mistake veterans make. When they are asked about their rank, they sometimes answer with their grade. No one knows what an E-5 is, but everyone knows what a sergeant is, or at least they think they do.

"Let me speak military to you. You have to be able to translate your MOS (Military Occupational Specialty) into its civilian equivalent. I can help with that.

"That brings me to another thing: for good or bad, people have impressions about veterans. It's based on urban legend, movies, books, what have you. So let's look at the good.

"Veterans are disciplined. They know how to follow instructions. They don't argue. They are mission-focused. They understand the big picture. They are reliable. They are honest. They are trustworthy. If they were anything other than privates, they are leaders. They can give orders. They get the job done. They don't have to be micromanaged. They are hard working. They focus on the team and not the individual. They are problem solvers. They are decision makers.

"*Now I have made that statement to scores of veterans and, with the exception of Marines, they all laugh and want to tell me stories about officers they had.*"

"*Marines never say anything negative about other Marines.*"

"*I know. And I also know that the description I just gave is accurate for most, but not all veterans. But civilian employers think that is what they are getting when they hire a vet.*

"*On the other hand, they have concerns. The first is medical. Is this guy going to go nuts? They will never ask the question. For one thing, it's illegal. The most they can ask is, 'Is there any reason why you would not be able to perform the required duties?' But they'll be thinking it. In your case, you have an advantage as you have a visible disability. You have a slight limp. So when you tell them, and you should, that you had a medical discharge, explain what happened and what that means. But do it humorously. Don't tell them the story you told me. Just say, 'My best friend shot me in the knee. It ended my military career, but not our friendship. I'll never have to buy a beer again!'*

"*That way you show that you have a sense of humor, that you are not bitter, and that you're a nice guy. But then explain if there is any special accommodation you need.*"

"*The only problem I have is that I need to be able to stretch my leg if I am sitting at a desk for an extended period. So as long as there's at least four feet between my chair and the wall, I'm fine.*"

"*Perfect. So now it is not an issue.*

"*Now for the bad. The other thing that comes up all the time is supervision. When I tell a client that the veteran had supervisory experience, they immediately disregard it. They think that all 'military supervision' means is barking orders. They don't understand the process.*"

"If I had just barked orders it wouldn't have been Joe who had shot me!"

"I know. But explain it to me."

"Whether I was supervising two men or twenty, I told them what our objective was and then we would discuss the plan. Sometimes we had to do it my way. Usually we tweaked the plan. Everyone had to be comfortable with it. And it couldn't be too complicated. When the adrenaline is flowing you can forget things. Forget something and you make a mistake. Make a mistake and someone dies or loses an arm. I served two tours in Iraq and one in Afghanistan. I never lost a man to enemy or friendly fire. I did a lot of training. That was my specialty."

"OK. Write this down:

"'Trained recruits (supervisory experience).

"'Perfect battlefield safety record.

"'Proven decision maker and implementer.

"'Proven team builder.'

"Those are all bullet points that we'll put at the top of your résumé under 'Selected Accomplishments.' But before we start writing, I have another question:

"Why did you decide to get a job and not go to college?"

"I don't have anyone supporting me. I figured with my benefits, I'd get a job and get a degree on-line or at a night school."

"Makes sense, but there are a lot of crooks out there so make certain the school is properly accredited. If they are offering you credit for your military service, let's say more than a year, be very suspicious and check them out."

"I was actually thinking about the University of Phoenix."

"They are certainly accredited and have a good reputation. Your plan is smart, but don't mention it to employers. They might think you will not be focused on work. Since it's something

you would do after hours, it's none of their business. But if they ask, and they might, tell them the truth.

"Now let's prepare a résumé. You do the writing:

"At the top goes your name, and you can put 'USMC' after it. If someone has a problem with it, you wouldn't want to work for them anyways.

"Underneath goes your address, cell phone number and e-mail address.

"Next comes 'Selected Accomplishments.' Here are the points that I mentioned.

"Now 'Work Experience.' Put down, 'United States Marine Corps, Gunnery Sergeant, 2005-2011. Then give a few bullet points about what your responsibilities were. You'll send me the draft and we'll work on it.

"Next comes 'Awards and Honors.' What do you have?"

"Around twenty."

"List them all. Anything that civilians will recognize?"

"Bronze Star."

"You might want to start with that one and also make it the first bullet point – excuse the pun – for 'Selected Accomplishments.' What are you going to say when they ask what you did?"

"I'd be happy to tell you but then I'd have to kill you."

"Good answer. Just make sure you smile. By the way, state secrets aside, it's not good for you to talk too much about your service. You have to build relationships with your colleagues. They will want to understand, but they won't and since you don't have anything in common with them, you might be building a wall around yourself."

"I've already noticed that when dating. Girls like to date Marines, but don't like to hear war stories."

"That's actually a good analogy. Job hunting is like dating. But there is one big difference. The entire job search

process is all about the employer. You have to meet the employer's needs, he doesn't have to meet yours. You have to convince him that you are the answer to his needs. Until he's confident that you can solve his problems, it's a one-way conversation – figuratively speaking."

"So what do I do?"

"After the pleasantries, and before he has a chance to ask you to tell him about yourself, ask him, 'What can I do to make your life easier?' I got that question from a friend of mine, Barry Cohen, at CUNY. He's their Employment Coordinator. It's the best question you can ask."

"Sounds simple enough – and effective."

"OK. We have your name and contact info, Selected Accomplishments, Work Experience, Awards and Honors. What about Special Skills and Languages?"

"I'm fluent in Spanish. And have a good command of French."

"Nice. Put them under 'Languages.' But what about 'Special Skills?'"

"Nothing that a civilian would be interested in!"

"How are you with computers?"

"I work with Word and Excel."

"Make it 'Special Skills and Languages' and list all four.

"I realize this is not the case today, but it will be. Anything that can differientiate you from your competition is important to include so, when you have them, add sections for 'Media Citations,' 'Publications,' and 'Speaking Engagements.' All of those speak to the fact that you are a recognized expert or authority in your field.

"And, this might sound silly, but have you done any volunteer work?"

"As a matter of fact, I volunteer at my church. I run an after-school sports program."

"So now we add 'Community Service' and with that we are finished.

"Now comes the hard question: What do you want to be when you grow up?"

"I don't know."

"When was the last time you were proud of yourself?"

"When I got shot I was teaching a green recruit how to use his weapon. This kid was a nervous wreck. Most of us didn't think he could make it. But I saw something in him. All he needed was discipline, structure, and to know that he was not alone."

"Sounds like you saw a bit of yourself in him."

"Exactly. I kept on telling him that I believed in him. The obstacle course, the physical demands, are killers. He had the strength; the problem was stamina and a lack of confidence. Then I got shot.

"I fell over, right beside him, and was screaming. This kid all of a sudden turned into a Marine. He took the strap off of his weapon and used it as a tourniquet. He yelled at me to stop rolling, which I couldn't do. He ordered – and I mean 'ordered' – the other recruits to hold me down so I would not do any more damage to my leg, and yelled at another Gunny to get help.

"Now I don't remember any of it, but that's what they told me. They also told me that at one point, when I was about to lose consciousness, he slapped me. He thought that it would be dangerous if I passed out."

"So what happened?"

"They reported to the Commander what happened. He called the squad together and he had Jack step forward. In front of everyone he yelled at him for striking me, told him that he had no authority to order a Gunny around, said he didn't want to see him on his base again until the following Monday, and made him a corporal."

"Promotion and a, what, 10-day leave? Not bad."

"And you know what?"

"He was more excited about the leave than the stripes."

"How did you know?"

"When it comes to some things, 18-year-olds are 18-year-olds, whether they are recruits in the Marines or the Israeli Army."

"I forgot you had told me on the phone that you served in the IDF."

"OK. So you like turning kids around. Why not do it professionally? Work with at-risk youth."

"How would I go about doing that?"

"The key to finding a job is really networking. The vast majority of jobs are not advertised. Ask your minister if he knows of any openings."

Jeff did. The minister didn't. But I did.

Sometimes it's better to be lucky than good. A few days after I met with Jeff I got a call from a non-profit that works with at-risk youth. The foundation of their program was sports activities. They contacted me hoping that I might know of a veteran – someone who would not be intimidated by the kids and who the kids would respect.

I'll let you guess what happened...

Oh, and the lesson: hire a vet!

LESSONS LEARNED

THROUGHOUT THIS BOOK I have taken a non-academic approach. Instead of playing lecturer, I have chosen to play storyteller. But now is the time for the lecture:

I honestly and truly believe that if you follow the lessons of this book you will get a job. There are no guarantees, but I am confident that my approach will work for anyone in any situation.

Here are the lessons for each section of the employment search process. Repetitions are intentional:

Job Search
1. Never forget that the job search is not about you, it's about the employer.
2. The key to getting a job is differentiation.
3. Make certain you are looking for the right thing. Sometimes you do not need a new job or a new career, just new responsibilities.
4. Attitude is everything.
5. Network with everyone you know – even persons with whom you have not been in contact for years.
6. Follow-up with anything your networking partners request.
7. Look for "shadowing" opportunities.
8. Only apply for jobs for which you meet the minimum qualifications.
9. Apply for jobs as soon as you hear about them. Don't procrastinate!
10. Employers only hire professionals, not amateurs.
11. Take advantage of all opportunities.
12. You are the only one responsible for your job search.

13. Graduate high school or, better still, college.
14. Never underestimate the importance of luck.
15. Be productive despite long-term unemployment.
16. The more people who know about your search, the less confidentiality you have.
17. Keep detailed records of your job-search activities.

Cover Letter
1. Don't obsess over the cover letter and résumé, obsess over the interview.
2. Differentiate yourself from the competition by keeping your cover letter short, sweet and to the point.
3. If your presentation is sloppy, it's a sign that your work will be sloppy. No one hires sloppy candidates.

Résumé
1. Differentiate yourself from the competition by starting your résumé with 'Selected Accomplishments.'
2. It's the quality of the résumé that counts, not the length.
3. Never lie.
4. All experiences are important.

Interview
1. Ask, "How can I make your life easier?"
2. It's not what you say that counts; it's what people hear that matters.
3. Research the employer, the interviewers, and the senior staff.
4. Be comfortable, confident and composed.

5. Employers only hire people they like.
6. Make a personal connection with the interviewer.
7. Attitude is everything.
8. Shake hands with the receptionist and interact with her professionally.
9. No negativity.
10. It's not the crime that kills you, it's the cover-up.
11. Never lie.
12. Never badmouth a former or current employer or colleague.
13. Remember "I vs. We."
14. Don't preach or sound presumptuous.
15. Keep your answers short, sweet, and to the point.
16. Listen! Listen! Listen!
17. Always follow-through.
18. Give only professional references.
19. Thank the interviewer at the beginning and end of the interview. Send a thank you e-mail and a hand-written thank you note.
20. A good thank you letter can save an interview.
21. Take responsibility for your interview failures and use the e-mail thank you to make corrections and clarifications.
22. Express interest in the job.

Negotiations
1. Be prepared for background checks - criminal, driving, drug, and credit.
2. Inform employers of negatives before they find out from other sources.
3. Be aware of your Internet presence.
4. Make certain your voice-mail message is professional, not silly.

5. You can only make one counteroffer, but it has to be based on needs, not wants.
6. Only quit your job when you have a written offer of employment, and give notice equal to your annual vacation time.
7. Do not accept a counteroffer from your present employer.

ABOUT THE AUTHOR

Bruce A. Hurwitz, Ph.D., President and CEO of Hurwitz Strategic Staffing, Ltd., became an executive recruiter in 2003, after a successful non-profit career. He started HSS in 2009, as a boutique executive recruitment firm specializing in permanent placements across sectors and offering career counseling services. HSS's mission is to promote the hiring of veterans of the U.S. Armed Forces and Merchant Marines.

Hurwitz is a recognized authority on recruitment, employment, and career development, having been cited in over 300 articles, appearing in more than 200 publications, nationally and internationally, including *The Wall Street Journal*, *USA Today* and *US News & World Report*, and on such websites as CareerBuilder, Monster, The Ladders, and Yahoo! The host of *Bruce Hurwitz Presents*, a live call-in radio interview program on BlogTalkRadio and an Ambassador for the Manhattan Chamber of Commerce, he also hosts the Chamber's weekly radio show, *The Voice of Manhattan Business.*

Hurwitz is an on-camera talent for eHow.com and is certified as an "Approved Career Expert" by CareeRealism.com. He teaches Professional Development and Professional Business Development at The Mechanics' Institute of The General Society of Mechanics and Tradesmen of the City of New York, and is an advisor for Purzue, the online multimedia résumé showcase for job seekers and employers.

An honors graduate of the Department of International Relations of the Hebrew University of Jerusalem, where he received his doctoral degree, he is the author of two books and scores of peer-reviewed and journalistic publications, and is a sought-after speaker on employment and career-related topics.

INDEX

www.ingramcontent.com/pod-product-compliance
Lightning Source LLC
Chambersburg PA
CBHW060018210326
41520CB00009B/928